All We Are
Are Stories

Veronica Turiano

for Rita and Vince

CONTENTS

I'm empty and aching and I don't know why.
~ Simon and Garfunkel
"America"

RIGHT THERE WHEN YOU NEED IT

But then if you're so smart, tell me,
Why are you still so afraid?
~ Billy Joel
"Vienna"

"No going in the water for *at least* thirty minutes," her mother shouted to her as she walked away from the wreckage of another awkward talk about what it means to be a teenager, complete with curfews, mosquitoes and beach vendor hot dogs. "You'll get a cramp and drown!" The more distance she got, the more her mother began to shrink, looking a little less like the ogre that she was, while Carl, her mother's boyfriend, looked more and more like a cow on its back picking hay from its teeth with its hooves. "Did you hear me?" her mother shouted.

With a dismissive "Yeah, whatever" hand up in the air, she turned the volume on her Walkman up all the way. "*Every breath you take,*" sang The Police, "*I'll be watching you.*"

She walked along the beach, her soles smacking and sucking the wet sand with kisses. She'd walk as far as her feet were willing to take her, as far away from her mother and Carl talking about breakfast buffets as she could go. Waves of foamy water washed over her feet, tickling her toes, before running back into the ocean without her, leaving behind tiny holes in the sand where little hidden mouths blew bubbles. Chewed-up bits of shells pricked her skin. She felt sorry for the clams who'd lost their homes, but at least they were free, she thought. At least they were allowed to swim. She walked until she couldn't see her mother or Carl anymore, and everything, even the sun, felt cooler.

She was beginning to change color. She could just tell. In the four days they'd been at the beach, she had only gotten what Carl had said was a darker shade of pale. It was her mother's fault for making her wear so much sunscreen. She had nothing but a pair of uncooked breadsticks for legs, Carl had said. Plump beads of wet slid down the thick grease of her knees. Nothing could penetrate. But now, finally, she caught a whiff of the air she'd been longing for. She knew because she smelled like coconut macaroons instead of Noxzema. She knew because the marshmallow knobs on her shoulders were roasting and soon her skin would be fire.

As she approached the private part of the beach, she thought about what Carl would say if he knew she'd wandered this far away, that she'd gone where she didn't belong. They'd driven two days to get here. And for what? To be trapped in a room together in that awful, grodie motel and parked on the same square of sand day after day? She didn't care what Carl would say. She'd walk forever if she had to, as far as she could. "*Every bond you break,*" sang The Police. "*Every step you take,*

2

I'll be watching you."

And then she saw them, the only two other people on the private beach, a boy in Ray-Bans with a boogie board tucked under his arm and a girl in a pink bikini stretched out on a blue and white blanket. Her kind of people. Not her mom and Carl and all the other flip-flopped people staying in their motel, with their bug-eyed smiles and one-piece suits with wads of fat shoved inside, the bulges that escaped showing off the red and white marks of yesterday's attire. As she moved closer and closer into the danger zone, silent houses lining the beach opened their big window eyes and looked back at her curiously. With every step she took, their eyes grew bigger and wider.

"*Oh can't you see,*" sang The Police, "*you belong to me?*"

The girl in the pink bikini was staring at the sky with her eyes shut. The boy was looking at the ocean. He was crouched down by the water's edge, listening, as if the water had something to say.

"Heya," she said to him as she slowly approached from behind like a shaky snake. "Any waves today?"

The girl in the pink bikini flipped over.

"Nah," said the boy. "Been pretty lame-o all summer."

"They'll kick up soon," she said. She had no idea if that's something people might say about waves, but she couldn't take it back now. It was out there. She tried to cover it up by saying something else. "Sure is a scorcher. I'll bet you could fry an egg out here." That was even worse. That was something Carl might say.

3

If only the waves would cooperate. Then maybe she could sit on the beach and watch him spin, flip and fall off his boogie board until it was time to go back to making sandcastles with her mother and Carl, who always stomped on them in the end, pretending he was Godzilla and talking like an Oriental person, saying things like "How you like that flied lice?" Carl was okay sometimes. But she hated when he would do things like that, or when he would pretend he knew things he didn't, like Algebra or who shot JR. He'd always brag about the time he'd played poker with a senator's son, but it was a senator no one had heard of.

A wave rolled over her toes and left something cold and slimy on her feet. It looked like a bit of harmless, icky seaweed, but then she noticed it had tentacles, and there was a barf-like substance oozing out of its mouth. She shook her foot, and the thing flew away and plopped, lifeless, on the sand. "Ew, gross!" she said. "What is it?"

"That's nothing," the boy said.

"But look at it," she said. "I've never seen anything like that before." She wondered if it was from another planet, or maybe it was something that hadn't been discovered yet.

"Could be," said the boy. "There's billions of different things living in the ocean. Who knows?"

"I think it's dead," she said.

"If it isn't," said the boy, "it will be soon." Then he kicked it back into the water.

The girl in the pink bikini sat up and said, "Hey, jerk, go get me a Mountain Dew."

4

"Go get it yourself," said the boy.

The girl stuck her tongue out. "Go on," she said. "And get one for your friend here too."

"Cat. My name's Cat."

"Hello, Cat," said the girl in the bikini. "Get a Mountain Dew for Cat, jerk."

The boy walked off, saying, "I'm only going cause I'm thirsty."

"You're probably thirsty too, right?" said the girl. "I mean, it's like fucking Hades out here."

Cat smiled. She didn't know what Hades was, but she sure was thirsty all of a sudden.

"You live around here?" said the girl.

Cat nodded. She hadn't meant to, but she did. "Well, not *right* around here," she said.

"That's our house there," said the girl, referring to one of the curious houses where the boy had gone, down a landing that stretched like a tongue into a big white mouth. "I'm Jackie," she said "That jerk's my brother, Jack. Is your name really Cat? As in the animal?"

"Well," said Cat. She could feel Carl's eyes on her now. Go away, Carl! "It's actually Katherine, like the actress Katherine Hepburn. I was named after her. But everybody calls me Cat. With a C," she said again. She held up her hand like the letter and then made an A and a T with both hands.

Jackie squirted some Bain de Soleil on her copper-toned arms. "Neato," she said. "My name's so lame. I was named after my grandmother."

Cat dug her toes into the sand. They felt safe down there. Sometimes a wave would smack against her ankles and splash her legs. Sometimes it would barely touch her at all. It was a secret little game of tag they played. The water seemed afraid to get too close or linger for too long, just in case she was able to catch it. Cat was almost certain she could.

And then a hermit crab poked its eyes out of the sand between Cat's feet. She jumped back and screamed. The hermit crab hurried back into hiding, and Cat said, "Oops. I think I scared the shell off it."

"You scared the shit out of it," said Jackie. Both girls laughed.

By the time Jack turned up with their Mountain Dews, the girls had made friends with the crab. They named him Ally Oops. They watched him scurry from one hole to another, eyes first, peeping along slowly, awkwardly dragging around the borrowed shell on his back that was two sizes too big. Cat said he looked like he was wearing a fur coat, like an old movie star all frail and boney inside. "I can barely hold myself up, *dahling*," she mimicked. "Look at my gorgeous mink and my big Bette Davis eyes," she said, batting her lashes. Jack and Jackie rolled around in the sand holding their stomachs. "Go away now, please," said Cat. "I vant to be alone!" And then they were all laughing together so loudly, Cat thought maybe her mother and Carl could hear it.

When the waves finally kicked up, Jack did some spinners on his boogie board. Cat and Jackie went in over their heads and got their hair wet, and Jack grabbed at them with his hands, trying to make them think he was a shark. Jack turned on his boom box and moonwalked in the sand. The girls huddled together, limbs dripping, under Jackie's blanket. It was the two of them against the chilly wind. "Fetch me my mink," Cat said in her celebrity crab voice, and they all started laughing again, laughing endlessly, until they finally surrendered to the lull of the ocean and drifted into a siesta of sweet dreams. Soft breezes came and went, passing over them like feathers. The sun reached down and hugged their slender bodies, and the waves danced, and the seagulls sang, and Michael Jackson whispered something about human nature in their ears.

As soon as she opened her eyes, Cat could see Carl and his fat belly in the distance coming towards them. He was wandering up the beach through hordes of screaming children with plastic donuts around their waists and stepping over people lounging out under umbrellas. He was looking for something. Cat knew what it was. He was getting closer. He'd be angry if he knew how far she'd gone. He'd shout and say embarrassing things. She had to escape. She had to get away before Carl ruined everything.

She ran back down the beach, leaving her new friends behind her, sneaking off like Ally Oops, peeping and hurrying, looking for a hole to hide in. She'd come back. She'd make up some excuse tomorrow, some reason for running away.

"Kathy!" Carl shouted through his megaphone hands. "Kathy Murphy! Where are you?"

People looked at him and then looked away. Cat looked away too. She hated the sight of him. She stood hidden in a crowd of children jumping and splashing in the waves, her back turned so she was looking out at the ocean. She couldn't find the end of it. She thought it made sense that people didn't always think the world was round, because it's hard to imagine things you can't see. She'd done a report on gravity for school once. "If you can't stand on a Ferris wheel without holding on," she'd written, "how can you stand on the earth without falling off? Because gravity's right there when you need it!" Her teacher had given it two gold stars and hung it up on the achievements board for everyone to read. But now, it finally made sense to her.

As Cat stood her ground on the big, round world, the waves smacked against her legs and tried to drag her with them into the endless ocean. A little boy wearing a snorkel ran past her and screamed as he hit the edge of a wave. His mother laughed, picked him up, and said, "Did the water scare you?" in a gentle baby voice.

"Kathy!" Carl shouted behind her. She wished her breadstick legs would run the other way. Not back, but forwards, into the future. Not here. Not now. Not with Carl right behind her. "I've been looking for you for half an hour!" he said. "Your mother's had an accident. We have to go. Now!"

Cat's mother had stepped on a piece of broken glass like a clumsy cow and needed four stitches. By the time they left the hospital, Cat's hair was bone dry and her stomach growled with frustration. Carl ordered some room service and they watched reruns of *All in the Family* while they ate. Carl decided that they should just go home the next day, two days early, since her mother's

8

stitches meant they couldn't go back to the beach. "I'll buy us all some Carvel when we get home," he said in an attempt to make Cat stop her moaning. "With extra sprinkles."

"But I didn't get to say goodbye," Cat said as they packed up the car, Carl's puke green Chevy Chevette with the broken AC and back windows made for children that didn't roll down all the way. Cat had to be stuffed into the back seat with all the luggage and beach gear spilling out of the hatch.

"To who?" said her mother.

"My friends," said Cat. "I won't ever see them again."

"What friends?" said Carl.

Cat groaned.

"Why don't you listen to your Walkman?" said her mother.

"You don't listen to a Walkman," Cat said.

"Then what do you do?" said her mother.

Cat groaned again. "Where is it?" she said.

"How should we know?" said her mother. "It's your Walkman. You're the only one who plays with it. Or whatever it is you do with a Walkman. No one knows what you do these days."

"It's not back here," said Cat.

"Didn't you pack it, Kitty Kat?" said Carl.

And then she realized. It was gone. Her mother and Carl had given that to her for her thirteenth birthday. She'd be in big trouble if she told them. She must have left it on the beach. Jack and Jackie were probably looking after it for her, waiting for her to come back and get it.

"Jackie's already in junior high," Cat said as a diversion.

"Jackie?" said her mother. "Jackie who?"

"My friend Jackie," said Cat. "I met her on the beach yesterday. She has a brother named Jack and they live here. On the beach. But only during the summer."

"What's she talking about?" said Carl.

"You got me," said her mother.

There was a congestion of cars going the other way, but they breezed right down the highway in the puke green Chevette. "Don't they know they're going the wrong way?" said Carl, snorting a bit as he chuckled. Whenever they hit a state line, Carl made them cheer. "Only three more to go!" he'd shout. "We'll be home before you know it!"

"Not at this speed," Cat groaned. She thought about opening the door and jumping out. If she had a sister, they could run away together. They could go back to the beach, find Jack and Jackie, go into the smiling house for Mountain Dews. Maybe they'd even be adopted. But she was trapped in this hatch alone.

Carl turned up the radio when Elton John came on. "*I'm still standing, yeah, yeah, yeah,*" he sang to Cat's mother because of her foot. Her mother only pretended to be mad about it. Cat looked away, but even then, it was hard not to see them, Carl with his sunburnt clown nose and her mother's bandaged foot with the fat swelling out. There were so many other people she could be riding with. Why did she have to be in this car?

Warm wind snapped at her through the window.

She stuck her hand out and tried to grab on to it before Carl yelled at her to get all her extremities inside. She watched the other cars passing them by. Who was in them, where were they going, and what were their lives like? She saw an old man and woman with a little dog wearing a red bow in its hair. A man driving a pickup truck was picking his nose. Another man was changing a tire while his wife and kids sat under some trees drinking sodas. Cat counted how many hours until they got home, how many days until school started, and how many years it would be until she could drive herself back to the beach, and she wondered if it was true what her mother had said, that real people don't live in two houses.

COLUMBIA

The dark goes before the dawn,
Open up your eyes.
~ Journey
"Someday Soon"

The quarter rolled through the phone with a *ting-ting-clink* as it landed in the return. Again: *ting-ting-clink.* And then finally: *ting-ting-tink* — and nothing. No dial tone, no cordial voice on the other side. Just the hollow sound of silence.

"Fuck! God damned stupid fucking useless piece of shit!"

Cassie smashed the receiver down and kicked the phone booth door. The man standing outside in the rain who'd been waiting under his big umbrella for her to finish making her phone call shuffled away nervously.

"Yeah — well, fuck you too!"

It was still raining hard. There was a crack in the sole of her right shoe where the rain had seeped in, and her sock was soaking wet. She would have covered her foot up with a plastic bag, but Marty's didn't use bags. People hauled their goods off in cardboard boxes, many

12

of which had been left behind in the rain, where they wilted and got run over. Cassie couldn't think of anything else she could put around her shoe to keep the rain out. Her only salvation would be in making that phone call.

She was cold, tired and hungry. She only had seven minutes left on her break, which was the equivalent of three and a half cigarettes. Her second break wasn't until 12:30. All breaks were rigorously scheduled by some unseen member of management. First and third breaks were only fifteen minutes, but the second one was thirty. If she had to pee before her 10:30 break, she was shit out of luck. One of the other smokers had warned her on her first day not to drink anything before or during her shift. It saved a lot of trouble and time when one needed to make the most of those minutes. A lot of people brought sack lunches with them to save time. Marty's sold food, but it came in bulk, and the employees didn't get enough of a discount to make buying five pounds of chicken salad even slightly appealing. Cassie didn't have any food at home to bring in, so she made do with the little packs of Chips Ahoy and Cheetos from the vending machine. Sometimes, she felt so weak from hunger she'd almost faint, and she'd grab hold of her cash register for a moment between scanning car tires and gigantic tins of tuna fish to keep from going down. The smoking didn't help any with the faintness, but it helped with the hunger. Smoking was like eating hate, sucking in the deepest breath of anger, and blowing it back out as *thank fucking god*.

Cassie kicked the phone booth door open and ran

for it, speeding past several rows of parked cars. The rain was heavy and sounded like a ton of bullets shooting down. God was firing at them. A god who hated cars. And parking lots. And wholesale retail warehouses selling one-gallon jugs of A-1 Steak Sauce. Cassie's kind of god.

The smokers all gathered under an awning near the garden center. Cassie had only been working there three hours by the time she'd become a familiar face under the awning. And now it was three months, and no one felt the need to acknowledge her anymore. Not that anyone really had. One or two of them had introduced themselves, asked where she'd come from and if she went to McNally's on Friday nights like everybody else. Cassie didn't know McNally's. She didn't tell them she was from another part of the Island. She just said where she was living now. She said she was only working at Marty's for the summer, saving up some pocket money for when she goes away to school. She drew a line and dared anyone to question it. "Where're you going, Smartypants?" they'd asked. She hadn't decided yet, she'd said. Somewhere upstate, though. Not around here. "Good for you," they'd said. "Do something with your life."

Marty's was a plain beige building the size of a warehouse. Its parking lot was bigger than Giants Stadium. Along the side of the building, there was an old, warped picnic table under a big green awning, something the garden center had donated so people could sit down while they smoked and ate their packed lunches and not get rained on. A fat girl named Tammy, who had gone through training with Cassie, but who had already been fairly well acquainted with everyone at Marty's through some nepotistic connection, was parked at the picnic table with a box of Twinkies and a can of Diet Coke. Cassie tried to make eye contact with her, but the girl looked away.

Cassie sat down at the picnic table and lit up a cigarette. She blew smoke into the air and watched it hang awhile before it was pulled away by the wind into the rain. She knew there was a Golden Pantry down the road somewhere. She tried picturing it in her mind so she could locate its pay phone, make a plan. She could run down there on her lunch break. She started to calculate how long it would take.

"You can use the phone in the break room," said a coarse, harsh, tannish woman named Darcy. She came closer to Cassie, puffed on her cigarette, and said, "I saw you over there. They really need to put a sign on that thing or something. OUT OF ORDER. How hard is that? How many quarters did it pinch you for?"

"Just one," said Cassie.

"You can make one personal phone call a day," Darcy said. "But it can't be longer than ten minutes. And you need to log it on the wall."

"If you don't log your calls," said an oily woman named Leslie, "someone rats you out and you get a misdemeanor. Then they stick you on the naughty step."

"Don't listen to her," said Darcy. "There's no naughty step. But you will get written up."

"Three strikes and you're out," said Leslie. "That's if they don't like you. If they like you, you can have as many strikes as you damn well want."

"Just be sure to log it," said Darcy.

"Thanks for the 411," said Cassie. She tried again to make eye contact with fat Tammy, but the girl looked away.

With three minutes to spare, Cassie slipped herself through a family of five, negotiated a complex pattern of cardboard boxes, darted past the cheese spread sample lady and a ten-pound bag spill of sugar in aisle twenty and made her way into the break room, where someone else was already on the phone.

"Fuck," she said silently.

She went to the bathroom and peeled off her wet sock. She held it under the hand dryer until parts of it were warm. If she'd remembered her boots, things would be so much better. It felt good slipping that sock on over her cold, craggy skin. It was the only thing that had made her feel okay that day.

At 12:47, she went back into the break room. She wrote her name, her employee number, and the time on the wall. She dialed a number so committed to her memory it had become a part of her DNA.

"Hello?" said her sister's small voice. "Who's calling, please?"

There was a thump in Cassie's heart, a punch of sorrow she'd not been expecting. She wanted to erase the past three months and everything they stood for. But only if she could rewrite it, too.

"Hello?" her sister said again. And when Cassie didn't speak, couldn't say a fucking thing without the chance of crying, her sister hung up.

"Fuck," said Cassie. She had to push the little buttons in the cradle twice before she got a dial tone.

Someone was depositing coins into one of the vending machines. Cassie paused. She didn't know if this warranted another log on the wall, and if so, she would have to wait until tomorrow to make another call. The name on the log was Cassie Donohue. But she wasn't Cassie Donohue; she was Cassandra Anna Marra. Her mother had been a Marra once. That was before she got married and turned into one of the pod people and, together with her father, plotted Cassie's death. Marra was her true name, she'd insisted, and she wanted it back. Who could prove that dickhead was really her dad? She didn't have his baldy head and squinty, gray eyes. She'd never been asked if it was okay with her, if she'd wanted to be a Donohue. She was old enough now to make the decision for herself. And if she was old enough to do that, they'd informed her, then she was also old enough to get the hell out.

And so she did. It had been three months now, and Cassie knew that one day it would be six months, three years, six years and then forever. But today, in this moment, she wanted time to peel away until the only thing left was that one time when she and her sister were holding hands in church as they sang Christmas carols, the time Grandpa Marra came to stay until he died and ushered all of them to midnight mass, both girls so hopeful about the promises of the next day.

It didn't count. They'd been disconnected. She dialed again.

"Hello? Who is this, please?" said her sister.

"Tara — it's me. Don't hang up."

"Cassie? Mommy, it's Cassie! Cassie — when are you coming home?"

"I don't know. Listen, put mommy on the phone for me, okay?"

"Come home soon, Cassie, please. I really miss you. Mommy says I can move into your room, but I don't want to. I want you to be in your room."

"It's okay, Tara, you can have my room. Just don't mess with my things. Keep your little fingers off my records. Okay?"

"What about your Barbie box?"

"You know where it is?"

"Yeah. It's on the top shelf in your closet. I can't reach it. But if you tell mommy that I can play with your Barbies, she'll get it down for me."

"You can tell her for me. But take good care of them."

"I will. I promise. Here's mommy. Bye!"

It felt too easy, hearing Tara's goodbye. If she'd died, she wouldn't have been able to hear what it sounded like. Maybe it would be more gloomy, more full of aching and regret. Less focused on the prize of Barbie and Ken.

"What do you want, Cassie?" said her mother.

The thump returned. This time, it felt like a whack full of hatred and neglect. "I need to come home for some things," she said.

Her mother sighed. "When?"

"As soon as possible."

"You can come tonight after supper."

"No. Not when *he's* there."

"Really, Cassie, I don't know why you have to make such a huge drama out of everything."

"I'm off tomorrow. I can get a lift from Brionne. It won't take long. We can come in the morning. Brionne has to be at work by twelve."

Another sigh from her mother. "I've boxed most of it up, so you'll have to tell me exactly what you want."

"My boots, maybe some clothes, and my records."

"Fine. What time?"

"Eleven."

"Fine, Cassie. Goodbye."

"Wait!" Cassie shouted. She couldn't risk having to make another call. The first one hadn't counted, but she'd be pushing it now. She waited a few seconds, hoping to hear her mother's voice again.

"What?"

"Have I gotten anything in the mail?"

"No."

"You sure?"

"Yes, I'm sure. Are you expecting something? Something from your name-changing legal team, perhaps?"

It was a dig that hurt, because it exposed the truth Cassie liked to mask with indifference, that her mother thought she was joke, and that Cassie's removal from the house was not entirely by choice. No matter how she formed it, it always ended up looking the same. But it was necessary, she knew, these steps she had to take on her own, in her own shoes, in a direction she was able to choose.

"Schools," said Cassie. "I sent out a bunch of applications two weeks ago."

"Schools? And how do you plan on paying for that?"

"Financial aid. Student loans. Job money. I'll do it."

"Uh-huh," said her mother. "And if that doesn't pan out? What? You expect us to pay for it? You still owe us for the car you wrecked. I don't think you understand how expensive cars and college educations can be, Cassandra."

"Then I'll come up with something else. I'll get two jobs. Whatever."

"Your plan is to go to college *and* work two jobs? You don't have the discipline to do one thing at a time. What school do you think is going to accept you with your bad record?"

"What do you know? I made good grades."

"Until you were expelled for drinking and smoking in the woods."

"What does that have to do with my grades?"

"You have a permanent record, Cassandra."

"So what?"

"You're being ridiculous."

"You're being fucking ridiculous!"

Cassie finished with a slam, the phone hanging half-cocked from the shock. She'd forgotten where she was. A room full of disgruntled labor powered by Slim Jims and Diet Sprite judged her and then looked away, rolling their eyes. What did she care? She was already done with this place. As soon as she earned up enough money, she'd quit. She'd move upstate, get a job in a bookstore or a café, enroll in a junior college until she could transfer. These people weren't her people. It didn't matter what they thought.

The rest of the day passed in a blur of twenty-pound bags of dog food, ten-gallon tubs of olive oil and slowly corroding cardboard boxes with various logos branded on their sides. Big, empty boxes full of processed cheese. She spent her third break under the awning, smoking other people's cigarettes. The fat girl, Tammy, who didn't even smoke, complimented Cassie's old, ratty denim jacket. Cassie told her it was vintage, mostly because she wanted to know if Tammy was dumb enough to believe it. She asked Cassie what she was going to major in. Cassie told her she was torn between History and Philosophy, which sounded really interesting by the course descriptions in the catalogs. Tammy said she could never do good in school because reading put her to sleep, unless it was *People*. Then Darcy said she was forty-two and still celebrating her high school graduation. "I couldn't imagine going back for more homework and all that shit," she said. "No thank you."

And then Cassie saw a family of four escorting their haul from Marty's to a silver minivan. Walking past them, on the way into Marty's, was a mother and daughter holding hands. It didn't seem to matter to any of them that it was raining. Even walking through puddles, they looked warm and dry: almost perfect. But they were fake. Poseurs. Cardboard people. They probably all had boring lives and lived in white-shingled houses and had no idea who Jimmy Page was or anything.

At 5:30, Cassie stood in the rain and waited for Brionne, who was always late. Cassie didn't know what she would have done without Brionne, or if she would have found the balls to stand up for herself without her. They'd been in the same Brownie troop as kids, and they'd been friends ever since. Brionne's dad was always drunk, and her mother died when she was ten. Cassie's father wouldn't let her go to the funeral. The only guilt Cassie ever felt was because of Brionne, for the possibility of leaving her alone in their apartment with only their landlady, Mrs. Bauer, to look after her. Mrs. Bauer was a frizzy-headed woman who'd gotten herself stuck somewhere in a different decade, and whose daughter had been a former beauty queen. The girls both adored and feared Mrs. Bauer. One minute she'd been calling down to them to come join her for a home-cooked meal, and the next she'd be reprimanding them for burning too many candles. Mrs. Bauer's basement had been the way out, but it was only a parking space, and Cassie wondered if leaving Brionne behind would somehow trap her in that void, where they were always welcomed by the rank smell of a thousand years' worth of cat piss lingering in the limp shag carpet that adorned their subterranean abode. Today was no different, but it did make the fangs of guilt bite a little deeper, as Cassie was determined not to be swayed by the bad vibes of her bitch of a mother. Her plan was clear: to escape from Marty's and the Bauer void by the end of summer.

"You tell your mom about school?" asked Brionne.

"She's such a cunt," said Cassie. "She said I was being ridiculous."

"Fuck her," said Brionne. "So what if you were?"

"I wasn't."

"Yeah, I know."

They smoked a bowl and stretched themselves out on the nappy shag pile floor with their legs in the air, their bare feet resting on the wall, pushing it away.

"Who the hell puts up paneling anymore?" said Brionne.

Cassie laughed as Brionne's words repeated in her head, only funnier and stranger each time, seeming more ridiculous. Ridiculous. Redikilish. Redickulush.

"You know what you should do?" said Brionne. "You should apply to fucking Columbia, get a fancy degree and some high-paying job, make gobs of money, wipe your fucking ass with it and give it to your parents for Christmas."

Cassie laughed. "Yeah, right," she said.

"I'm being totally serious," said Brionne. "You could do that."

"Oh Brionne, don't be riduckyluss," said Cassie through tears. The smoke was burning her eyes.

"You're so gone," said Brionne.

Cassie tried to get up without falling. "Fuck her," she said. She put on *Houses of the Holy* and let the music take control. "Columbia," she said, as if trying to make it real. "Columbia. Columbia."

"Yeah," said Brionne. "Columbia."

"Cassandra Anna Columbia."

They got to Cassie's house around 11:35. Brionne waited in the car as Cassie navigated the puddles on the walkway, her denim jacket hovering over her head. As she stood on the porch ringing the bell, she noticed how sharp the bushes were, how unwelcoming the slate that wrapped around the house and the fence that shut out the backyard must seem to anyone who didn't live there.

No one was home.

"That stupid bitch," Cassie said when she got back in the car.

"No way," said Brionne. "You think she forgot?"

"No, I don't think she forgot. I think she's just a stupid fucking bitch."

"Yeah, that's probably it."

Cassie found herself sitting in front of the phone in the break room again a week later. It was her 10:00 break.

"You weren't home."

"You were late."

"You could have waited."

"I have a life, Cassandra."

"What about my life?"

"Did you call me just to aggravate me?"

"I need my things."

"After dinner."

"No! I told you. Not when *he's* home."

Cassie's mother sighed. It was a big, exaggerated, "I want you to feel this" sigh.

"We can be there tomorrow at 11:00."

Another sigh.

"Please."

Silence.

"Mom. I need my things. My shoes are pieces of shit and I've been wearing the same two pairs of jeans and Mrs. Bauer only lets us use the washing machine for two hours once a week and I can't afford another pair of shoes and my feet are always wet and cold and those are my things and you'd said when I left I could come back for them and I tried to but we were late because Brionne couldn't find her keys and then we had to stop for gas and I tried to call you but the phone wasn't working—"

"Fine, Cassie. 11:00. But please don't be late again."

Tara opened the door and shouted, "Cassie's home! Cassie's home!"

"I'm in here, Cassandra," said her mother's voice from the living room, which was cluttered with cardboard boxes. Her mother was sitting on the sofa with an unlit cigarette and an envelope in her hands. "Syracuse?" she said. "You've got some dreams, kid. Not only do you think you can get in with your SAT scores, but you're damned and determined to get as far away as possible. Aren't you?"

"What's it to you? Just give it to me."

"Have you even thought about how this is affecting your sister?"

"I don't give a shit."

She was sorry she'd said that. She was already sorry she came. Tara wasn't in the room, but she had good ears. Tara never missed a beat. It didn't always make sense to her, but she wasn't living in bliss by any means.

25

"Tara can come and live with me as soon as she wants. Can I just see the letter, please?"

"You didn't get in."

"You opened it?"

"Of course I opened it. It came to my house."

Cassie kicked one of the boxes and lifted its lid. "Are my boots in here?" she said.

"So how many other little envelopes should I expect?"

Cassie ignored her. She kept her back to her and rummaged through the boxes, pulling out pieces of clothing and tossing them on the floor.

"What about my records?" she said.

Her mother lit her cigarette. She turned her face away and looked out the window at the rain.

"Tell me," said Cassie. "Where are my records?"

"Your father put them in the trash. Along with your posters and whatever else you had hanging on your walls."

"He did what?" But the thought of it rose inside of her like a flood. Every sense of hope had drowned. "Those were *my* things! Mine!" She felt disgusted. "Why? Why are you doing this to me?"

"I don't know what to do anymore, Cassandra," said her mother. She was still looking away at the rain. "I give up."

Cassie kicked the coffee table, but it barely nudged. She kicked it again. And again. And once more before using the heel of her holey shoe to give it a slam. And then she felt her arm going behind her, pulled by something physical, something much stronger than her.

It was her father. She'd been tricked!

"Get out of this house now," he said, pulling her towards the door.

"Let go of me! Let go of me!"

"This is how you behave? This is my home you are destroying," he said through gritted teeth.

The doorbell rang.

"Andrew, please," said her mother. "Let me handle this."

"I want her out of this house," her father said.

"Just let me deal with it."

Her father let go. She didn't look at him, but she knew he was gone, probably back into the kitchen where he'd been hiding like a sniper. Cassie could hear Tara sobbing under the dining room table.

The doorbell rang again. Then there was rapid knocking. Cassie's mother opened the door.

"Hi," said Brionne cheerfully. "Is Cassie almost ready?"

"Just a minute, Brionne," said Cassie's mother. "I'd just like a moment to speak to my daughter."

"That's cool," said Brionne. "I'll wait in the car."

Everything was blurry. There were tears building up in Cassie's eyes.

"I honestly don't know what to do anymore, Cassandra," said her mother. "I have done everything I could for you. I've tried everything. I can't do it anymore."

There was no controlling it. Tears and the strains of her muffled weeping took control of Cassie's face. She wanted her mother to hug her, but the thought of asking for that made her face go even tighter. Besides, those days were gone now. In the corner of her eye, she could see Tara's crying eyes hiding behind her hair under the dinning room table.

"What's your plan?" said her mother.

Cassie caught her breath. She wiped the water off her face. "What do you mean?"

"Supposing you do get into one of these schools, what do you intend to do?"

"I don't know yet," said Cassie. "But you don't think I can get in anyway, so—"

"No, Cassie. No. That's your interpretation. But I want you to be realistic. I don't want you to be disappointed. You have a history of giving up on things. Ballet. Piano. Tennis. First you wanted to be a hairdresser. Then it was Pat Benatar. Then a forensic scientist. You don't know what you want."

Brionne blew her horn.

Cassie grabbed her boots. "Thanks for nothing," she said as she walked to the door.

"You're no angel, Cassandra," was the last thing she heard her mother say before she was gone.

Brionne was waiting for her by the car. "What the hell, Cassie?"

"We need to get the fuck outta here, like, now, or I'm gonna go fucking ballistic on his ass."

As soon as they were in the car, Brionne booked it down the street, slamming on the brakes at the first stop sign. "You okay, Cass?"

Cassie cried.

"You're better off without them. You'll see. You're gonna save up lots of cash, get into Columbia, become a famous philosopher."

"No, I'm not."

"Maybe not. Who knows? But you're gonna do something. Even if it is just that guy from the 7-Eleven. It's like what Nina Simone said. *Ooh, child, things are gonna get easier...*"

Cassie looked at Brionne blankly.

"My mom used to sing that to me."

"That's not helping."

"Alright then. How about Pat Benatar? *Well you're a real tough cookie with a long history...* Come on, Cassie girl!"

"*Hit me with your best shot...* motherfucker!"

Brionne stepped on the gas and they were on their way again, voices in harmony, in control, indestructible.

"Look out, Columbia!" Cassie shouted over the chorus of their collective lives. "Here I come!"

Many weeks later, Cassie found herself fully ensconced in the social life under the awning at Marty's. She'd given up the idea of college, not because she'd lost interest, but because there'd been no news from home since the day she and Brionne had driven off with her boots, and at Marty's, there wasn't much to aid her escape into her philosophic fantasies. She'd saved up enough to legally change her last name, but she and Brionne used the money to throw a party instead. They'd settled into a decent routine in the apartment and had divvied up the chores. They bought a groovy lamp for the living room and took turns reading passages from a copy of *Naked Lunch* Cassie had borrowed from a new guy at work Cassie dated for a month. Brionne made casseroles on Sundays that would get them through half the week, and along with the occasional bratwurst from Mrs. Bauer, the fainting spells soon subsided. Her feet were warm, and the cardboard boxes faded into the fabric of her life.

Things under the awning at Marty's became routine, too. She and Tammy would share cream cheese and jelly sandwiches, pudding cups, Diet Cokes and the occasional acne remedy. Cassie knew by now that Tammy was the daughter of a very popular woman who'd worked at Marty's for ten years, but that she herself had lacked the poise required to sail through puberty without capsizing. The poor thing had been left floating in the water for too long, which was how, Cassie assumed, she'd gotten so bloated. Cassie felt obligated to save Tammy from perpetual adolescence and virginity. Tammy needed rescuing. Cassie, however, was a pirate; she took control under her own terms and abandoned ship only at her whim. She'd only recently abandoned Kris, one of the floor managers, after they'd gone down to McNally's together a few times. Cassie could feel he was getting too clingy, so she told him things were going too far, too fast. She had her eyes on Neal's friend Matt now. But still, she'd admired Kris's excellent work ethic, something she'd been able to mimic just enough to get her off the tills and into payroll, a move that came with a two-dollar raise. It was in the caged-in confines of the payroll booth where Cassie learned she was still pretty good with numbers and fantasies of college life occasionally carried her through the duller days of counting change.

And then Cassie found herself in the break room one day writing her name in the log on the wall: Cassandra Donohue, with hearts instead of As and Os. And when her sister said, "Hello? Who's calling, please?" Cassie said nothing, because she knew that neither one of them owned the vocabulary to express what they'd needed to say.

And then the rain returned. Summer was over and things fell from trees and settled, air became crisp, and life in Mrsbauerland was decorated with overflowing ashtrays, dirty dishes and books Cassie had borrowed, but never returned.

And then, not long after autumn set in, as Cassie sat under the awning listening to the heavy rain, waiting for Brionne to come and get her, she saw her mother's car lurking in the distance. It had come to a stop at the edge of the parking lot, right next to the broken pay phone. It did nothing for a while, then it drove away, Tara's sad face staring back at her from the rear window.

A few days later, Mrs. Bauer called down for Cassie to come and collect a letter that had been dropped off for her that day. It was in a large white envelope with "SUNY New Paltz" printed in big, bold letters in the upper left-hand corner. Cassie opened the envelope and scooped out the insides delicately, slowly devouring the images on the bulky course catalog.

"Holy shit, Cass," said Brionne. "Maybe you really did it. Maybe you actually got the fuck in."

The photo on the cover of the catalog had already sucked her in. She was already there. She was sitting on the steps of a silky white building with the high pillars, flanked by newly formed friendships and the promises of tomorrow. She was stretched out in bed in her dorm room reading Kerouac. Posters of her two favorite bands hung on the walls and a milk crate for her new record collection sat neatly in the space between her desk and the door. They would all be looking for her at Marty's, but she wouldn't be there, wilting away with the abandoned cardboard, waiting for her ride, perched like a lazy bird on the picnic table. She'd be gone soon. She'd be free.

"I knew it," said Brionne. "I knew you'd do it."

Cassie stared into space. She saw herself again, on that day when her mother and Tara had driven away, when all she could think about was getting into that car and going away with them, even though she knew it would mean giving up a lot of things, that it would be hard at first, that it wouldn't be perfect. She could see herself there, sitting next to her sister, like that Christmas they had held hands with that feeling it gave her. She didn't know what it was, but she remembered how much she had wanted it.

CRASHING

I'm tired of the talking,
I know what you're about.
~ My Morning Jacket
"Into the Woods"

It was one of those shitty situations that couldn't be helped because he'd let some asshole, some junkie he didn't even know — a friend of a friend's friend — crash in his loft. And now, just because of a single, teensy-weensy, minuscule and, really, when you think about it, wholly inescapable slight lapse of judgment, he was on a train going east, going backwards, going home.

"You said 3:25," Court said soon as she saw him. She'd been waiting for over an hour. She'd left the kids in the car, and one of them, Jamie, the middle kid, had puked out the car window after sucking on six packets of Sweet'N Low.

"Never mind the hell I've just been through," said Sean. "How the fuck are you?"

Court walked ahead of him, leading the way, trying to force him to pick up the pace. Down the platform steps. Across the parking lot. Over the anger. Through the resentment. Back to the beginning. Sean and his

33

duffle bag and his roll-along suitcase full of wrinkled clothes trailed six paces behind her.

They stopped at the puddle of vomit.

"I can't believe you let your kids eat that garbage," said Sean. "*You* of all people."

Court opened her trunk. "Hey, kids, it's Pot and Kettle time!" she said. "Tell me, little Sean Mulligan, do you know where the big hand goes when it's 3 o'clock?"

"So I missed a train, so what? There's always another train."

"You couldn't call me and let me know? You've got to leave me here with three starving kids, one of whom thinks he's a vacuum cleaner."

Jamie and his big sister, Josa, glared at them through the rear window.

"So I took another train. Jesus Christ. Relax."

"There won't always be another train, Sean. I won't always be around to pick you up." Court slammed the trunk shut. The strap to Sean's duffle bag hung out like an emergency pull cord.

"Good to see you too," he said.

"Don't," she said. "I've got three kids to worry about, a job I hate getting up for, a blocked toilet and a suspiciously missing Raggedy Ann. I can't do all this white picket fence crap and rescue my kid brother from the crack house."

"Wow. I really pissed you off, didn't I?"

"Four years, Sean. You got four years. This is what I got."

"F you."

"F you too."

34

"And thanks for picking me up."

"You can thank me by not bringing any of your junk into my house."

"I'm junk free these days, remember?"

Court reached into the back and pulled a naked Barbie out of Jamie's mouth. "Oh yes," she said. She stabbed the ignition with her key. "What was I thinking?"

It wasn't Sean's fault that Court had gotten knocked up during her first and only year at Juilliard. Sean didn't knock anyone up, so he got to go to Pratt. That was the deal. And it wasn't that Sean didn't like the hairless monster that had pushed its way through Court's business. On the contrary, from what he knew of her, he quite liked the kid's tender cynicism and bitter joy. She also played a mean game of Donkey Kong. But it wasn't his fault. That had never stopped Court from hating him for every success and failure he'd managed to pull off since Josa had popped her head into the world nine years ago.

Court started her engine. It kicked up and then died. She tried again. "Useless piece of shit," she said.

"Mother!" said Josa from the rear.

"Sorry," said Court. The engine caught. She gave it some gas. Josa and Jamie cheered.

"Really," said Sean. "Thanks for picking me up, sis. It's mighty scary in da crack house."

They went home. It was them again. Still them. Always them.

"So what the fuck were you doing with all that shit anyway?" said Mitch, Court's new old boyfriend.

They were sitting around Court's kitchen table eating cold Arby's roast beef on a bun.

"It wasn't mine and don't ask," said Sean.

Mitch was Josa's dad. He'd been replaced for six seasons by a guy named Glen, just like the dad in *Bewitched*. They looked a lot alike, but Glen was a realtor. When Sean had come back from a year of living dangerously in San Francisco, he eventually noticed that Mitch had gotten shorter. But that was because it was Glen. Glen was Jamie and Eddison's dad. Sean didn't know how Court had gotten rid of Mitch or why the hell he'd come back, but he was glad to see him. He hadn't cared too much for the other Mitch. He wore way too much fucking khaki.

"Think you can paint a house?" said Mitch.

"He can paint anything," said Court. "It's *will* he paint a house?"

"I can paint a house," said Sean.

"I need someone who's good with color," said Mitch. "Got a client who wants me to match a pillow. Job's over in Merrick. You can drive in with me in the morning, take a look at this pillow."

Mitch had wanted to play bass for Pearl Jam, but as that never happened, he'd taken a job painting houses instead so he could support Court and Josa. Now he was also supporting the other Mitch's kids. He was either a saint or stupid. Sean figured buying the company he'd been working for was just one of the many things Mitch did while he'd been on hiatus.

"Cool," said Sean. "When you say 'morning'…"

Court gave him a kick under the table.

Court's house was a constant violation of creative space. It was a prison sentence with non-stop Nickelodeon. There were the everyday fights over slices of pizza and unwanted farts, along with the occasional slapping battles that Josa — bigger, stronger, older — always won. "She outranks you, buddy," Sean would say to a crying Jamie. "You'll never win. Take it from me." Baby Eddie would watch all the chaos from the safety of his highchair, oblivious to the power struggle he would soon become a part of, happily nesting in a cocoon of his own crap that gave off a fetid reminder of his presence. One day, he'd get his too.

By Sean's calculations, Court's house was only about a block away from where his old tree fort used to be. He'd conquered the world in that tree fort. He'd defended a helpless nation, made fire, eaten squirrel (that was really a Nathan's hot dog) and perfected his art of thinking, fiddling with himself for hours. Back then, he'd had potential, possibilities, a bright future, all that stuff. Now he was crashing on Court's sofa, not really sleeping, but staring at walls and eating stale Lucky Charms in the shit town he grew up in, wondering what the fuck comes next. He'd gone full circle, in a squiggly line kind of way. He was only alive now because he wasn't dead yet.

"Think you'll stick around this time?" Mitch asked him after three days of daytime TV, old yearbooks and after-dinner games of Clue. Jamie had swallowed the lead pipe, so they had to use a pretzel stick instead.

"Not sure," said Sean. "You?"

Mitch let a few moments pass, in which he poured

half a warm PBR down the drain. "Hard to say," he said. "Not really up to me."

Back in the living room, Josa was showing off her jetés. "This is fifth position," she said. "And this is a plié." Mitch and Court applauded, even though they'd seen it all a million times before. Sean didn't know a plié from a jeté, but they'd been a part of his life for as long as he could remember. Josa even had the same long legs as Court, and both of them wore their hair straight and let it hang over one side.

While Josa was twirling around in circles, Court started to cry. Then Jamie came running into the room wearing his Superman costume and Court's black suede boots, shouting, "Kill the evil ballerina!"

"Oh my God!" said Josa, her hands clenched in claws of frustration. "He's so freaking weird!"

"Revenge of the middle child," said Sean.

Court got up and left the room.

Sean had only been in the middle for four years, which might have been enough time for him to earn some psychological terminology that made him part of a statistic he'd choose to ignore, but it was the lack of the third child that had really thrown him off base. He wouldn't deny that one.

"You ever wonder what it'd be like if he was still around?" Sean said to Court a few nights later when it was only them left in the living room after Mrs. Peacock killed Professor Plum in the conservatory with the pretzel stick. "I mean — what if he hadn't fallen into that pool? Would we be different?"

"Seriously? What's the point?"

"Maybe you'd have gotten along better with him. You guys might have been close. You could've had someone else to push around."

"Give it a rest, Sean. You always do this. You always bring up Patrick like he's some kind of dark matter pushing us apart. It's late. I'm going to bed."

"You wouldn't have needed Josa."

Court turned off the television. The glow of the table lamp cast a harsh, dim yellow hue over the room. "I never *needed* Josaphine," she said.

"What are you saying? She was an 'accident'? That's bullshit, Court. You can't be happy unless you have someone to control. Seriously, you should wear more black, because I think the audience can see you."

It had happened on her watch. It was summer. Sean always remembered eating ice cream and the lawn sprinklers being on. The rest of it had been filled in over the years. The cat's fleas, the kitchen table stacked with plates and cups on the back patio, the pesticide bomb Sean worried would blow up the house, and Patrick being gone, Patrick being face down in the neighbor's pool, not breathing when they'd finally found him. Court had been given the order to keep her eyes on him, but there was a fight over a quarter — twenty-five fucking useless cents — and in the midst of this, the third one had snuck away. How he managed to reach the gate latch was uncertain, and myths surrounded it like shadows on a grassy knoll. But it didn't matter. He was gone.

There were supposed to be three. That was supposed to be them.

A few months into his sentence of sofa sleeping,

Court woke Sean up with some news. "Hey, you remember Josh? He's got a studio."

"Josh? Josh who?"

"You know — Josh who I used to go out with, Josh."

"Right. That Josh. What about him?"

"He's got a small studio up in Queens. He might be willing to let you in there, but you'll have to go see him. Show him your stuff."

While Sean was in rehab, Court and Mitch had rented a U-Haul. They salvaged what they could from the loft. There was a storage unit. Sean hadn't been in it yet, but it was time. Court wasn't going to pay rent on the unit forever.

"I'm sorry — did you say something about Queens?"

"You really want to spend the rest of your life painting houses to match pillows?" She handed him the keys to the storage unit. Then she gave him the keys to her car. "Drop the kids off at school before you head out. Take the train. Leave the car at the station. Mitch will pick it up."

"Maybe I don't wanna do this."

"Oh, *I'm* sorry. Did I forget to mention I don't want you living on my sofa for the rest of your fucking life?"

Sean didn't have choices; he had circumstances. He'd needed the extra cash to pay off a loan from one of those quick credit-at-a-price places so he could pay his rent, but then the cash ran out and he couldn't pay the rent or the loan payment. The junkie had promised him some pills and a hundred and fifty bucks. He never did get the cash. What he got instead was an uncomfortable night in jail and six weeks in a psychiatric ward with a middle-aged man who liked to play with his penis, a teenage pathological liar, a really fat nympho, a skinhead with an imaginary llama and a Chinese klepto named Fuck Cluck or Chuck Fuck or some shit like that. Court had made all her choices sober and with the soft cushion of Mitch's paint-speckled arm to lean on.

There was a train at 2:05. That gave him plenty of time after dropping off the kids to get over to the storage unit and get his portfolio together. Court told him he could spend the night in the city, he just needed to make sure the kids got to school on time. After that, he could do whatever he wanted. There was only one other stipulation. He knew what it was.

When they got to the school, Josa didn't get out of the car. "I don't go here," she said.

"What?"

"This is regular school. I go to the Davenport School."

"The Davenport School?"

"It's Montessori. It's over near the high school. You were supposed to drop me off first. I start at 8:40. Jamie starts at 9."

"Why didn't anyone tell me this?"

"Mom told you last night. You said something about the high school burning down. But it hasn't. It's still there."

It was still there. It was like opening a box he'd sealed the lid on ten years ago. Every thought, every emotion, everything was still in there: his first kiss, his first smoke, his first drink, his first fistfight. He remembered the way the art rooms smelled to him on his first day. He'd wanted to fuck that smell, to curl up inside its heady, linseedy warmth.

"That's it there," said Josa. "See? The Davenport School."

It looked like something little elves would live in, except it was roughly the size of a four-bedroom Victorian. "Why do you go here anyway?" said Sean.

"My grandmother pays for it. There's my teacher, Karen!"

"You call your teacher Karen?"

"She and mommy are friends."

Josa bolted out of the car and ran over to Karen. And then something else jumped out of Sean's box: his first fuck.

"Holy shit!"

Josa was pointing. Little elves were running around screaming. Karen was walking towards him. "I heard you were back in town," she said.

Sean wanted to set his box on fire. "Court didn't mention you were Josa's teacher," he said. "Wow. You're a fucking teacher."

"Unfuckingbelievable, huh?"

"You look good," he said.

"You look exactly the same."

Sean stayed in the car. He only rolled the window down halfway. "It's all the drugs," he said. "Stunted my growth."

A bell rang. Elves from every direction gathered together into a small stream leading into the building.

Josa waved at him frantically. He didn't know if she wanted him to save her or to say goodbye.

"She's quite a kid," said Karen. "Spitting image of Court."

"You've no idea."

"Well, I'd better get inside and do my fucking job. Was good seeing you again, though."

"Yeah. You too. Good luck with the teaching gig."

"Thanks. And hey, Sean, listen..." She put her hands on the car door. She leaned in closer, so that some of her mousey hair snuck in through the window. She still had tremendous eyebrows. "I'm really sorry about Court," she said. "You guys handling it okay?"

"It's not that bad," said Sean.

All the elves were gone. It was just them out there, Sean and Karen, Josa's teacher, Court's friend, his first fuck. "If you ever... you know," she said. "Court knows how to reach me."

"Yeah, okay," he said.

"I'm always around," she said.

"Well, I'll certainly give that a fairly decent amount of consideration," he said.

"I mean it," she said. "I'm here if you need me."

Karen waved goodbye and went back to the elf house. Sean noticed the way she'd sauntered, like a slow train with an empty caboose. From the rear, he never would have guessed she was the same girl whose thighs he'd once parted with his tongue. He wouldn't do it again. Karen wasn't the first girl he'd choose to bump into, but it made sense. Everything he saw these days was regrettable. He'd dumped Karen two days after they'd had sex because she'd said *Sixteen Candles* was better than *The Breakfast Club*. It didn't really matter, but Sean had said he could never love a girl like that.

He went to the storage unit and picked up his portfolio. Then he went to the Parkway Diner for some lunch before he had to catch the next train. As he was leaving the Parkway, some lunatic ran across the highway, jumped the brick ledge and tackled him with hyper, gangly arms.

"Sean fucking Mulligan!"

It was Tyler, his old smoking buddy.

"I thought that was you. How the hell are you, man? I swear on my life, man, we were just talking about you the other day. Me and Swifty and Tony Matteo. You remember little Tony? Yeah, man. Holy shit, this is awesome! I don't know why, but you just came to my mind, and I was like, 'Hey guys, I wonder what the fuck ever happened to Sean Mulligan.' Where've you been, man? What's been going on?"

"Not much. Just, you know. Just living out in Brooklyn."

"Yeah, yeah. You're still painting, right? Yeah, right. Holy shit, man! That senior art exhibit and the guy suspended from those hooks. I fucking remember that shit. That was intense. What was that?"

"My self portrait."

"Fucking classic, man." Tyler lit up a cigarette and offered one to Sean.

"Quit," said Sean.

"No fucking shit?" said Tyler. "Yeah, I need to start thinking about doing that myself. So tell me everything."

Sean said things had been pretty uneventful, nothing much to tell. He didn't bother to mention the catastrophic journey he'd just been on, the shit train that had driven him back home. There was an old lady walking her dog along the side of the highway. Tyler said something about how she aged every time a car whizzed by her and soon she'd be nothing but dust blowing in the wind. Sean couldn't remember exactly, but his best guess was that they were six steps away from the place he'd last seen Tyler. The wind hadn't blown very hard around him.

"So where're you off to, man?" said Tyler. "A bunch of us are going out to Quogue for the weekend. Some guy Diane's dating has a place out there. You remember Diane?"

"You used to fuck her?"

"Who didn't fuck Diane?"

The old lady's dog barked at them.

"She looked a little too much like Court for me," said Sean.

Tyler snapped his fingers. "That's it!" he said. "Your sister. I saw her about two weeks ago over at the hospital. That's what made me think of you. I can't believe I fucking forgot about that. How's she doing, man?"

"Court? She's fine."

"That's cool. Glad to hear it, man. Hey, you wanna come out to Quogue this weekend? There's plenty of room. Swifty's picking me up at four."

"What time's it now?"

"Hell if I know."

"Can't. Gotta go out to Queens."

"What the holy fucking hell do you gotta go out to Queens for?"

"A life."

"Well, if you change your mind, I'm living over in Eaglewood Apartments now. Building 13."

"Yeah, I don't know. I've really got to do the Queens thing. But maybe next time."

"You back for good or something?"

"Nah. Just a few more weeks," said Sean. "Did Court tell you what she was doing at the hospital?"

"You don't know?"

"She might have mentioned something."

"She didn't tell me anything. I think she was, like, just having some tests done. But even if I knew something, and I told you something, I don't know everything. You know what I mean? What I mean is, I think you need to ask Court about it, is what I'm saying."

Sean looked around for the old lady. She was gone.

"Give me a lift to my place?" said Tyler.

"Yeah, sure."

"*Excelente*, my friend! So, like... are you completely smoke-free?"

"Nah, not completely."

"Sean Mulligan — my hero."

Tyler lived in a maze of identical brown buildings with numbers as their only decorations. It was the last place Sean ever imagined Tyler would end up, but he figured it probably made sense for a guy like Tyler to want to slip into the mainstream and get lost. Tyler said he was the only one of their old crew still earning less than thirty grand, but none of them were happy. At least, not by Tyler's estimation. Nothing had really changed.

"You were lucky, man," said Tyler. "You got the hell out."

"I didn't get very far," said Sean. "Just spun my wheels a little."

"Well keep spinning them. This place will rot you."

The night the junkie had given Sean the pills, he'd seen his baby brother's corpse sitting naked in the street. Its rotting flesh slipped off when Sean grabbed hold of its arm. There was nothing underneath.

"Remember that night we saw those lights?" said Tyler. "I still wanna know what the fuck that was. Man, no one ever believes me when I tell them that story."

Sean didn't believe it either, and he was there.

"That's all we got, though, man," said Tyler. "Them stories."

The two of them sat there for a moment, in the fresh haze that filled Court's car, and listened to all the silent stories that told them who and what they were.

"Fucking Diane, man," said Tyler. "She had nice tits for a prima punk."

Sean laughed. He'd been thinking the same thing.

"So, Queens it is?" said Tyler.

"Queens it is," said Sean.

"That's cool, man. Far be it for me to begrudge a man his time in Queens." Tyler put his hand out. "Keep in touch?"

"Will do," said Sean.

They shook on it. Tyler hopped out of the car and

ran off in front of it, swerving around suddenly and coming back again to Sean's side of the car, motioning for him to roll down his window. "One more thing," he said, "I'm sorry about your sister." Then he ran away, turning back again only once to flash Sean a peace sign before he slipped into the maze and disappeared.

That was 1:43.

By 1:52, Sean was sitting in his sister's car watching people gather on the platform, waiting for the 2:05. There was a pregnant lady with a fake Gucci handbag, a man wearing a dark blue suit and some tremendous sideburns, and a mixed-race couple with a mishmash of shopping bags. They had destinations, destinies waiting for them on other platforms. They had potential, possibilities. It would be so easy to step on the gas and collide with them all. It would only take one little movement to change the world. What if this was their last train?

He distracted himself by riffling through Court's glove compartment: old receipts, a broken ice scraper, a plastic dog with a missing head and a collection of empty candy wrappers — one of which housed an old, chewed-up piece of bright blue gum. There were also a few cassette tapes: Sonic Youth's *EVOL*, Patti Smith's *Horses*, *Mickey Mouse Disco* and a mixed tape labeled "Songs that Kick Ass" that Sean had made for Court during the summer Goodwill had come for their dead brother's bed while they were away at camp.

He remembered that the first song on Side A was "Police and Thieves" by the Clash. He pushed the tape through the cassette deck slot in Court's dashboard. He rewound Side A to the beginning and pressed play. The unmistakable tinkle of Tori Amos's "Silent All these Years" came through the speakers, and then the sounds of a dying herd of cattle, and then nothing. He hit the eject button, but the tape wouldn't come out. It was dead, deck and all.

"Motherfucker!"

He waited for the arm of the railway law to go up, the ding-ding-ding of the bell and the flashing red light fuelling his memory of a song he used to know, a story he could tell when this one was over. He thought about all the words he'd probably never say.

He watched the 2:05 roll away. Then he pulled out of the station and headed home. Them again. Still them.

There'd always be another train.

This Is What You Want. This Is What You Get.

There's a gate and a fence and bars to protect
From only God knows what lurks outside.
~ Tracy Chapman
"Remember the Tinman"

They brought trays full of mole and maize bathed in queso, a bottle of tequila, some warm beer and a boom box that played Latin music. They called her "Señorita Janita" and offered her some of the flautas their wives had made. "Celebrate life, Señorita Janita," one of them said to her as he filled a paper plate with refried beans. She felt guilty taking food from them, even sharing some of their joy. How much joy could they afford when Jim was only paying them twenty dollars a day? And still they celebrated into the night as she watched through the window. And there was Jim, her husband, a man she hardly knew, ten inches taller than any of them, dancing and laughing and singing "La Bamba".

"No more soy marinaro... no more soy marinaro sauce, capitan, soy capitan, oy capitan..."

It was Jim's idea to convert the garage. Into what exactly, Janet didn't know. She'd said it was okay, as long as she didn't have to get involved, and provided they didn't touch anything else. This meant the old Chevy would have to sit on the driveway, its rust and rot and dirty oil leaking into the ground through the cracks in the tar. Jim went to the lumberyard and picked up some wood and a few Mexicans. They helped him push the Chevy out of the garage and block its wheels with the scraps of a 2x4 so it wouldn't roll down their steep hill of a driveway. In less than a week, the job was done, and the Mexicans invited a priest to come and bless the garage. And then they were gone, and the house went silent again, owned by death.

It had been going on for twelve years. Slowly. Surely. Stubbornly.

One day, as they passed each other in the hallway, Janet said, "*Last Picture Show* is playing at the dollar theater."

Jim stopped for a moment and closed his eyes. "Can't place it," he said.

They'd watched that film together. Twenty-six years ago. Her mother had been working nights. Janet had borrowed the tape from a girlfriend. She'd only known Jim three weeks. It had been a momentous occasion.

"I thought we might want to see it again," she said. But Jim had already retreated into his hideaway, his secret space in their two-car garage.

Since the renovation, the Jim she'd married had half departed, and a figure that looked something like him would sometimes come and go from the garage, pale and rumpled. Sometimes, he would be wearing only his underwear. Sometimes, the Jim she'd married would be there instead, standing over her while she attempted the cryptic crossword, offering alternatives to "Gnashing your teeth under the covers". Janet never knew which Jim it would be when she'd hear the deadbolt unlock. Sometimes, Janet would knock on the garage door to signal that dinner was ready, and one of them would eventually appear and take his plate away, leaving Janet to eat dinner alone in the den watching *Family Feud*. Sometimes, no one would come out at all.

And then the hoarding began. Newspapers, magazines and catalogs. The mailman would always give Janet a pleasant grin. He had no idea the things he was bringing never went away. Janet would stack the mail neatly on the kitchen counter, and one of the Jims would come and take it away. What did he do with all of it? There was no way to find out. He had the only key. And he took it with him everywhere.

What would she tell the neighbors? Two of them had children in her school, and one of them, Elizabeth Martin, was on her roster this year. They must have wondered about the renovations, and the Mexicans, and the mailman with his Santa sack full of JC Penney catalogs. What did he tell them? Fuck the neighbors. She had nothing to say to them anyway. She'd always kept a distance. She'd always needed it that way.

She shopped for one these days. She didn't know what he ate. She went to the movies alone. What he did to pass the time was a mystery to her. She didn't try to solve it. She just didn't know how.

And then, one day, there was Mrs. Martin at the

Shop 'n' Save. "Oh, hello, Ms. Bennett," she said. "I thought that was you."

"Yes, it's me," said Janet.

"Lizzy was very excited when she found out you were going to be her teacher," said Mrs. Martin. "She thinks you're a celebrity. Ms. Bennett lives across the street!"

"We're just ordinary people," said Janet. "Just people who teach. I'm afraid Lizzie would be disappointed."

"Oh, not at all," said Mrs. Martin. "Lizzie thinks you're married to Superman."

Janet hee-hawed. "Jim?"

"Yes, well, like all nine-year-olds," said Mrs. Martin, "Lizzie thinks every policeman is a superhero. My father-in-law was in a bad car crash a few years ago. He likes to embellish. When Lizzie gets an idea in her head..."

"I see," said Janet. "I'm afraid Jim's retired. He's not saving anyone these days."

"Retired?" said Mrs. Martin.

"Medical reasons," said Janet. "Superheroes can be very fragile."

"I won't tell Lizzie about that," said Mrs. Martin.

There was nothing physically wrong with Jim, and that was obvious. Until a few months ago, he was still out in the yard every Saturday morning trying to repair it from whatever disease it had that forced it to grow in clumps. He would spray it, seed it, water it and trim it with the weed whacker, but the lumps continued to pile up and rocks appeared in the gritty lava that pooled around them. Whatever he had been doing had only made it worse. Janet came home one day to find Lawn Doctor parked in her driveway. The next day, it was the phone company. The day after that, it was the Mexicans again, delivering an old, donated sofa to the man who had paid them beans.

"What do you do all day?" Janet had asked him once when he came to collect his supper.

"Things," he said before disappearing again.

Poor Lizzie Martin had no idea what she was up against. But she'd find out soon enough. She'd grow up and marry a superhero who would ignore her needs, leaving her to rot away in a silent house on a hill of knobby weeds. On the first day of school, Lizzie had given Janet a picture she had drawn of her house with the old Chevy on the driveway and Janet and Jim standing on the bumpy front lawn. Jim was wearing a cape and a big S on his chest. Janet wore a red dress, flats and a sad face.

"Now there's the sign of a happy occasion," said the mailman one Saturday morning. He handed Janet her daily stack. On the top was a copy of *Cricket*.

Janet waited patiently for Jim to come out and collect his mail. She sat at the kitchen table, thumbing through the Fingerhut catalog, and then the door to the garage swung open.

"The mailman thinks we're adopting," she said.

"Good for him," said Jim.

"You're reading children's magazines now? Are you that desperate for words?"

Jim gathered his magazines in his arms and his

bathrobe flung open. He wasn't wearing his underwear.

"Little Lizzie Martin thinks you're a superhero," said Janet. "She thinks you're out all day saving the world."

"I am saving the world," said Jim. "My world."

"That what you call it, your dingy hovel? Do you even get any air in there?"

"Of course there's air in there. It's not outer space."

"So you say."

"You've got a sense of humor like your dad, you know that?"

That was mean. Janet hated her dad, and Jim knew it. She went back to her Fingerhut hunting and Jim returned to his world with his mail and dead-bolted the door behind him.

And then Lizzie Martin got the chickenpox, and Mrs. Martin rang the school asking if she could visit Janet at home to collect Lizzie's schoolwork for the week. And then Mrs. Martin was at the front door, and Janet was begging God not to let one of the Jims out of the cage.

"This ought to keep her itchy fingers busy," said Janet.

Mrs. Martin smiled, and Janet decided she'd need to change dentists, as if a good set of teeth was the distinction between delight and dysfunction.

"The vocabulary list is in there, but I'm assuming she won't be in on Friday to take the quiz."

"I can quiz her myself," said Mrs. Martin. She hadn't invited her in, but Janet could see her eyes roaming about, bumping into things and tipping them over. Fortunately, Mrs. Martin, like most mothers, was easily distracted by her mother's pride. "Lizzie always gets hundreds on her vocabulary quizzes," said Janet. "She's my star pupil."

Mrs. Martin's eyes now flashed straight at Janet. "She loves quizzes," she said. "She likes teaching her new words to her dolls, and then she sits them at the kitchen table and quizzes them. They all pass, except for Rainbow Brite. She's got to use her red pen on someone, just like a real teacher."

Janet heard a noise behind her. "Looks like rain," she said.

"Some days, Lizzie wants to be a teacher," said Mrs. Martin. "Other days, it's roller skating queen or horse brusher. But my husband thinks she'll end up with her own talk show. She loves to talk."

Janet couldn't argue that Lizzie had a way with words, and she was often wont to use them, always first to raise her hand or offer some commentary on the lessons. When they had introduced the "Just Say No" campaign, Lizzie had asked for "specification" because some drugs were "advantous". She had written a short poem about the four food groups called "Minding Your Pees and Carrots". The only word she had ever gotten wrong on a vocabulary quiz was "misspell".

"She'll learn one day that what we want isn't always what we get," Mrs. Martin was saying, "but I don't want that day to come too soon."

Janet heard more noise. It was coming from the kitchen. "She doesn't need to do all that work," said Janet. "Just whatever she feels she can. And tell her I hope she's feeling better soon and that we all miss her in class." And then she waved and took a step back. She had just about shut the door when she noticed the smell. She didn't know what it was or where it came from, but it had probably been there the whole time, nudging at Mrs. Martin's coat sleeve.

"She must have wondered," said Janet the next time she ran into one of the Jims.

"Let her wonder," he said. "It's none of her business how we live. It's our own damn business."

"But is it necessary? Should we reconsider?"

"Reconsider what?"

"This."

"I don't get your point."

"I feel like you've turned your back on me."

She'd felt that way for years. He wasn't the only one who didn't get the point of 4th of July picnics.

"It's rubbernecking, Janet. Everyone's a rubbernecker. Don't matter what you do or don't do, blood or no blood, they're still gonna look. You can't control other people," he said before disappearing again.

It had been happening for years, the walls building up around them. They didn't talk about it. It was none of their business, what they did. She'd accepted that he'd been through a lot, that he'd changed, and their marriage had changed with him. But what about Janet? How had she changed? She wasn't athletic or clever; she couldn't bake, sew or sing. She'd tried to dance once when she was a teenager, alone in her bedroom with the door shut and the blinds drawn. "Breaking Up Is Hard to Do" by Neil Sedaka. She *doo doo doo down doo be do down* downed and twisted her ankle. Her doctor said she'd ripped the ligaments apart so much, she had only skin holding her foot on, so it was good hers was so thick. Jim did what his father had done; he put himself in the line of danger to serve and protect people he didn't give two shits about. And then one day something propelled him to drive around in the old Chevy looking for For Sale signs on people's lawns. They'd wanted more space so the space between them would be less crowded. When they bought the house with the little garden in the back, Janet said, "Let's grow some enthusiasm." But they'd planted nothing. Weeds sprouted and choked their passion. They invested in the stock market and went on vacation to places like Tijuana and Toronto. They had their shutters painted. They bought a new living room suite and hung a fake Picasso on the wall. Then Jim said he'd had enough suburban burn to turn him black, went back to growing his hair and stopped shaving, and Janet became another woman, an older, mustier version of herself. It was their own damn business.

Janet had been prepared for Lizzie's mother to turn up after school on Friday, but she didn't. When the doorbell rang on Saturday morning, Janet had expected to see Mrs. Martin's good set of teeth. But instead, a stern, heavy-lidded male face narrowed its eyes at her when she opened the door and said, "I'm Ben Martin, Lizzie's father."

"Oh yes," said Janet. She covered herself with her robe.

"I'm sorry to disturb you so early in the day," said Mr. Martin. "I have Lizzie's homework."

"Yes," said Janet. "How is she doing?"

"On the mend," he said. "But she won't be in on Monday."

"Yes, I figured that," said Janet. "I have some more work for her. If you wait here..." He had advanced towards the door, trying to get in, but Janet stepped back. "Just one moment," she said.

Mr. Martin smiled and nodded. Janet took the manila folder with Lizzie's homework into the kitchen and tightened the knot in her robe. When she returned with a new manila folder, she found Mr. Martin standing in her house surveying her own damn business. A stack of *Car and Driver* by the door. A box of unread newspapers on the stairs. The scent of human soil in the hallway.

"I understand your husband's retired," said Mr. Martin.

"He is."

"Some sort of injury."

"That's right."

"That his old Chevy in the drive?"

"Yes, it is."

"Because I noticed it's stationary."

"He blew up the engine about two years ago."

"He home? I'd like to speak to him about something."

Normally, usually, almost always, Jim was home. But not today. He'd gone out with the Mexicans the evening before and still hadn't come back. Janet knew this because she'd waited up for him all night, sitting on the sofa thumbing through a *Pennysaver*.

"Jim's away," said Janet. "His mother's ill."

"Sorry to hear that," said Mr. Martin. "I hope it's not serious."

"She's 91. It's always serious when they're that age."

"Of course."

When Jim's mother had really been ill, having had a stroke in the middle of the night, Janet had dropped him off at the train station. He'd gotten out of the car without saying goodbye, and she'd heard nothing from him for days. For all she knew, either Jim or his mother had died, and it had never occurred to Jim to call and let her know which one it was.

"Is there something you'd like me to ask him?" said Janet.

"No, no. It's just that... Well, something's occurred, and I thought I might be able to talk to him about it."

"Not something bad, I hope."

"Just some phone calls to the house."

"Prank calls?"

"I'm not pointing any fingers, Mrs. Bennett."

"If you tell me what happened, perhaps I can offer some advice. Being the wife of a cop, you pick up on a lot."

"Far as I know, it's only been happening recently."

"Have you reported it? Was it kids?"

Mr. Martin cupped the manila envelope in his hands and crossed his arms in front of him. "Not kids," he said. "An adult. A man. He's phoned my house on three occasions this week when my daughter has answered the phone. We've told her not to answer the phone anymore, but you can imagine, she was pretty shaken up."

"What kind of prank was it?"

"He told her he was watching our house. Said he could see her. Told her he's seen us, her mommy and daddy, naked in our bedroom."

Janet couldn't imagine what kind of sicko would say such a thing to a child. Who had the time to sit around and randomly dial phone numbers all day, hoping to hear a child's voice? Who'd be so awful as to think of such a thing?

"I'm not sure how this crackpot got our number," said Mr. Martin, "but if I find out who it is…"

"Yes," said Janet. "I can imagine how you feel. But I'm not sure how Jim can help. You should report it right away."

Mr. Martin had reported it, and the police had told him that these were usually not random cases, but people who knew who they were calling. If it continued to happen, they could change their phone number. But Mr. Martin felt the damage had already been done. Lizzie was having nightmares. They were only words, but they did unimaginable things to his daughter's mind. Lizzie had found it difficult to say anything since repeating the caller's words to her mother.

"He called a few times when my wife answered and just hung up," said Mr. Martin. "This guy knows what he wants."

"He's not going to stop. Not if he knows he might get her again."

"Anyhow, I just thought perhaps I could speak to

your husband about it."

"I'm afraid there's not much he could do. Being retired."

Mr. Martin handed Janet a card. "Can I just give you this? Just in case you or your husband can think of anything to say."

Janet slid the card into her pocket without looking at it. "I'll let Jim know about it," she said. "But, as I've already told you, he's retired now, and there's not much we can do to help you."

"All the same, I just thought I would mention it to him. I know he's home a lot these days."

"Yes." Janet shoved her hands down deep into the pockets of her robe. The hard edge of Mr. Martin's card pressed into her skin. "I'll mention it to him when he gets in," she said. A draft of cold slipped through the front door, and when Mr. Martin opened it, a gust of wind whipped at the robe around her legs and roused the newspapers and magazines in the nearby boxes. It had all made a kind of horror movie noise, a wind and paper symphony of screams and cackles.

"The detective I spoke to suggested it might be someone in the area, or someone who's been in the area, like a garbage collector, handyman or—"

"A mailman," said Janet.

"Could be."

"Did they have an accent?"

"An accent?"

"From another country?"

"I don't think she'd pick up on something like that."

"I'm just trying to help," said Janet. "I'm just trying

to think of who might have been in the area."

"Like I said, Mrs. Bennett, I'm not pointing any fingers."

"No, you're not." Janet grabbed the door and pulled it close to her. "Please tell Lizzie I hope she's feeling better soon."

She shut the door on Mr. Martin and the world and stood frozen and silent in the empty house that was growing around her, stealing her air and choking her. The smell punched her in the face now. And though it stank like rotten cheese, she knew it was not from the drippings of flautas meant to celebrate life. The knot around her waist dug into her stomach. Every bit of her was taut, her thick skin a barrier holding her in, containing her.

She fingered the card in her pocket, knowing that she could. In that stale, stagnant moment, she knew that she certainly could.

PEOPLE GOING DOWN

You have to learn how to die
If you want to, want to be alive.
~ Wilco
"War on War"

"Would you jump?" asked the woman sitting next to him.

"Beg pardon?" he said.

"If you were there. What would you have done?"

Teddy didn't know. He had slept through it. And he was glad about that. He didn't feel guilty or sorry or sad. He was grateful. Fucking delighted. In the days after it had happened, it was all people could talk about. There were photos in some of the newspapers of people falling. Or jumping. Escaping. Accepting. Who knows what? It wasn't the first time in history innocent people had suffered for the sake of the immortality of the lunatic fringe. The world had known real horror before. But it was the jumping people couldn't stop thinking about. That was just too much.

"Maybe," Teddy said. "If I was in the south tower."

"What difference would that make?"

Teddy didn't know the woman sitting next to him,

but they had a mutual acquaintance, which is how they came to be sitting on opposite sides of a sofa watching the news with the sound turned down. Because even though they'd seen too much, they still couldn't get enough. They need more; they need to know more, to feel more, to keep being more. People were mulling about somberly, drinks in hand, talking about how they felt, where they were, what they'd do. Some of them were coupled up or in groups guarding a corner of the room with slanted smiles on their faces where the fear crept in. They were celebrating the marriage of two people who'd come to the conclusion, after several long debates, that professing love in a time of such hatred was not the wrong thing to do.

"If you're in the north tower, you don't know," Teddy said. "You think there's a chance. If you're in the south tower, you already know there's no hope."

"Oh," said the woman sitting next to him. "I never thought of it like that. But I don't think it matters."

"Sure it does," said Teddy. "Have you ever considered jumping out a window? It's a lot more daunting than it seems. There's no guarantee. It would depend on your distance, but with enough room, you could get lucky, pass out before you hit the ground, but it's not an ideal way to go."

"No, I wouldn't think so," said the woman sitting next to him. Then she turned her attention back to the television and shut Teddy off completely.

The day after it had happened, Teddy had gone to visit his mother. One of the nurses had told him that they'd made the decision not to inform some of the patients of the news. It would only upset them, the nurse had said. It would just be too much. Sometimes, she had explained to him, family members withhold tragic news, so that some patients die without knowing they didn't go before someone else, someone they might miss or whose passing signaled the way out. It was like pushing someone off a boat just before it sank, she had said. So, if he didn't mind, Teddy was asked to support the staff and respect their request for keeping mum.

"Of course," Teddy had said. "No problemo."

It was the same nurse who had fit his mother with her morphine drip. Janine was her name. Janine who always wore red lipstick. In a kind "I don't judge, I just work here" sort of way, she'd said that many patients have visions and experiences, and it would be best for him not to question his mother's, should she have them. Teddy had been confident she wouldn't. "My mother doesn't believe in God," he'd told her.

"Sometimes," she'd said, "it's seeing loved ones who've already passed."

"She doesn't believe in them either."

Janine had patted him on the shoulder and smiled before she walked away, the way nurses do when they know words are useless. What can you say to a man who looks for a laugh at the foot of his mother's deathbed?

"Did they shoot the president?" his mother asked. "Everyone's so damn miserable."

"They're just miserable in general," Teddy told her. "It's a hospital."

"Well tell them to cheer up already. It's annoying."

When Kennedy was shot, people had the same

national grief on their faces. Teddy mostly remembered it only because his mother had constantly complained about it. "They have nothing better to think about?" she'd said to his father. "I'm supposed to cry for a man I never knew?" Teddy's father had told her not to mind it; it would be over with soon enough. People have problems of their own. It wasn't long after that when Teddy's mother went down to his school to complain about Teddy's teacher, the one he'd informed her had continued to break into sobs for no apparent reason. Teddy didn't know what his mother had said, but he assumed it was more of a "my child comes here to learn" lecture than a "childhood is a time for innocence" one. Teddy had asked his mother if he was supposed to cry too. "I'll tell you when to cry," his mother had said. But she never did. And now, on her way out of this world, Teddy accepted that she never would.

Janine came in to change his mother's saline bag. Teddy's mother made a face. She'd been in and out of it all morning, but in that moment, Teddy knew she was fully awake. "That one there," she said in a whisper, "always has tears in her eyes."

Janine with the red lipstick and the tears in her eyes.

Looking at her now bending over his mother to adjust her various tubes and gadgets, Teddy thought he could relate to a woman whose job it was to help people die. He also knew something about doomed goods. He owned what was once a thriving record store that carried mainly imports and things too obscure for Sam Goody. He'd managed to do fairly well for a while after the CD revolution. He'd refused to stock them, insisting they would blow over, just like the LaserDisc and the grief after JFK. But then the customers stopped coming, save for the occasional curious out-of-towner and a small handful of hardcore vinyl enthusiasts mourning the glory days of cyclical grooves and static crackle. They were knights-errant on an endless quest for audio perfection. Teddy hated the thought of having cold, hard cases in his bins, but the cold, hard cases had won, and he was nursing the store to its death very slowly.

They were alike, he and Janine. And they both liked red lipstick.

"I see your handsome visitor has returned," Janine said to Teddy's mother.

"This is my son," said his mother.

"She was bragging about you after your visit yesterday," said Janine.

"This is my son, Teddy," said his mother. "Not my husband. My husband's been dead since 1976."

"Yesterday?" said Teddy. Yesterday had been a Saturday. He'd worked all day in the shop and went home to bed afterwards. He hadn't visited his mother yesterday.

"My father died in 1948," said his mother. "It was Thanksgiving. Dropped dead in the gravy boat."

"She said she spent the afternoon with the most handsome man in the world," said Janine with the red lipstick and the nod in her eyes.

"My husband died in 1976," Teddy's mother said to him.

"I know that, Ma," said Teddy. "I was there." It was the Bicentennial, the year his father had died. Teddy remembered it well. He was twenty-one. It was the same year he'd discovered Pink Floyd. *Ticking away the moments that make up a dull day.* Yes, he remembered it very well.

"I've been alone since then," said his mother. "Someone needs to look after the baby."

Janine stepped out of the room and shut the door, leaving Teddy alone. He didn't know where his mother was, but he knew he wasn't with her.

They'd given her two weeks. Teddy was fine with that. It was enough time to do whatever he needed to do. He didn't know what that was yet, but he knew he needed time. Six days in, and the carnations he'd brought the day she'd started on the morphine drip had already turned brown. Someone had thrown them away. He didn't know how much longer she'd put up with it all: the itchy bed sheets, the orange Jell-O, the suspicious liquid percolating through the plastic tubes shoved into her arms. The pain. Teddy's mother had always been able to ignore pain. But not this kind. And he knew she wouldn't stand for it for too long. Teddy told her it was okay, she should just relax, try not to notice. It would be over soon enough. He could smell the rotting tissues of her body on her breath. He had to force himself to get close to her, to hold her hand. It was cold, limp and calloused. He would never have done that if she'd been in her right mind. "I'm here," he said. He didn't know why. His mother closed her eyes, one part of her hooked up to this world, one part in anticipation of another. She'd know it soon enough, the nothingness that follows.

"I'll come back tomorrow," he said. "With some fresh flowers."

It was early the next morning when he got the call. It was Janine.

"Do I need to come down and identify the body?" he said.

"No," said Janine. "We know who she is. But there's some paperwork and a few personal belongings."

"Of course," said Teddy. "I wasn't thinking."

His mother's things had been put into a large Ziploc bag with her name on it. It wasn't anything substantial: a tube of ChapStick, a pair of gold earrings, a photograph of his father before Teddy was born and a plain white envelope. Teddy remembered the earrings. They were the only pair his mother ever wore. The ChapStick had made no sense to him, but the nurse who'd given him the bag said someone would be held accountable if it went missing, and he could discard it himself. He'd seen the photo once or twice before. Circa 1950, he thought. His father leaning against the railing on the deck of a ship, cigarette in hand, the artificial horizon of Ellis Island floating behind him. If there was a story to that photograph, he would never hear it. It was irretrievable now. He put the Ziploc bag on his mother's kitchen table, where it became buried under old newspapers, mail and insurance forms containing details of his mother's life that he needed to go through before she could finally die.

Before she went into hospice, Teddy's mother had still lived in the second-story walk-up on Staten Island they'd moved into after his father had died. The man who owned the building, Eli, had given Teddy a month to clear out her things. That was enough time, wasn't it, to gather up enough Hefty bags and leave them on the curb. "There's a lady wants to move in next Saturday," Eli told him. "That makes four weeks." He was counting the week his mother wasn't living in her apartment because she had gone somewhere else to die. Teddy didn't argue with him. He knew all Eli would have to say was that he needed to make a living too.

His mother didn't hold on to things, so clearing out her place was not a very big job. It was mostly canned goods and boxes of oatmeal that he dropped off at the local soup kitchen, clothing and linens that he took to the Salvation Army, and furniture that he'd arranged to have them come and pick up. None of it was worth anything. The only personal items were in a folder marked "birth certificates". Teddy's was in there. So was his father's death certificate. And there was an envelope with a notecard that read "Greetings from Flatbush, ha ha ha!" and a recipe for Irish soda bread from his Aunt Edda, who'd died the same year Teddy was born.

"Life isn't easy, but it isn't the hardest part," the woman at the funeral home had said to him the day he went to arrange things for his mother. Teddy couldn't agree with her. He thought life was too intricate. It was too much like a group activity. But death was simple. It was singular. It was a one-time event. And then it was done. There were no more doctor visits, no more prescriptions to fill, no more discussions about leaky toilets and garbage men who come too early in the morning and then leave spillage all over the road. There were no more phone calls to make or to take, no more questions to ask. No more gradual disclosures to wade through. There was no more discomfort. No more pain. No more waiting.

Cleaning out his mother's place didn't provide Teddy with the closure he'd been told it would. It was just exercise, running up and down the steps with heavy trash bags. Even seeing his old buddy Jimmy didn't stir up any ghosts for him. Jimmy's mother lived in the building next door, though the two women had never become friends. Jimmy was sorry to hear about Teddy's loss. He'd not heard she was sick, but he wasn't around much these days, now that he'd been made partner in his law firm. Jimmy had a wife and two kids and a big house in Maryland. "I've turned into a Jew," he told Teddy as they stood on the sidewalk of their youth with a bag of Teddy's mother's shoes. "I'm very faithful. Money is intoxicating."

"I thought you were going to Boston to join the IRA," said Teddy.

"Didn't pan out," said Jimmy. "Law school kept me busy."

"Good thing," said Teddy. "Doesn't seem like now is such a great time to be a terrorist."

Jimmy said his wife had joined a support group. She didn't know any of the victims, but that didn't matter. Everyone needed support these days. "There's even one for spouses of people who can't cope," Jimmy said. "That one meets every Wednesday."

Teddy thought the best way to cope was to forget

all about it. Let those assholes vanish with the smoke and the ash. Infamy denied. Just let it go.

"If only it was that easy," said Jimmy.

Teddy laughed. "After all," he said, "tomorrow is another day."

"So I hear you're in the music business," said Jimmy. "Ever meet Mariah Carey?"

"Never heard of her," said Teddy.

"So you'll believe me when I tell you my wife looks exactly like her?"

"Yeah, so does mine," said Teddy. He thought about the red lipstick again.

There was a diner just down the street from the hospital, a regular hangout for nurses, orderlies and EMTs. Teddy had been in there once before, the first day his mother had gone into hospice. He'd needed a cup of coffee, a grilled cheese sandwich and some key lime pie before he could go back into the room where his mother lay waiting to die. He'd wondered if Janine with the red lips ever ate there.

She came in one day with another nurse, ordered a cup of coffee to go, and bought a pack of breath mints. Teddy bumped into her on her way out. "Oh, hello," he said. His mother had only been dead two weeks. He knew there must be something about his appearance that didn't seem right. But it was too late now.

"Back so soon?" said Janine. "Are you all right?"

"No, yes," said Teddy. "I mean, yes, I'm fine. Not that it hasn't been an adjustment. I mean, you know, forgetting she's gone. I mean — I keep driving this way absent-mindedly, you know, so I thought, while I'm here, why not grab some lunch?"

"I'm on shift," said the other nurse.

"Right behind you," said Janine.

Teddy held the door open for them. He followed them out. They stood on the sidewalk. They exchanged glances.

"Well," said Teddy. "Nice seeing you again."

"Take care," said Janine.

Two days later: same time, same place. Teddy said they had to stop meeting like this. She was with the same nurse, who now looked at him like he was some kind of creep.

"Janine looked after my mother while she was passing away," Teddy explained.

"Yes," said the other nurse. "She's quite good at that."

"Best nurse in the ward," said Teddy.

"Well, there you go," said the other nurse. "Better not keep her for too long then." Then she did that thing that nurses do: she smiled; she walked away.

"Sorry," said Janine. "She's just in a mood."

The next time, it was that she'd had a patient die. A young man. A father.

"Must be hard, dealing with that all the time," said Teddy.

"It's what we get paid to deal with," said Janine. "But yes, it can be."

Their conversations didn't get any longer. "Tough day?" Teddy would say.

And it was always "the usual".

This continued for several weeks. Then Teddy got a

phone call from Eli. "You left a sack of shit here," he said. "I keep it in the basement. You get it before next Wednesday, trash day. Yes?"

Teddy skipped lunch at the diner to go out to Staten Island. He stood on the stoop of his mother's old apartment building for twenty minutes, in the rain, waiting for someone to buzz him in. In the basement was a large shopping bag filled with newspapers from the week his mother had died, the week they'd been printing all those photos of the jumpers. Teddy thought he'd sent them all on their way to the landfill. He took the bag outside and sat it on the curb. An old lady walking an old dog snickered at him, so he picked the bag up and carried it to his car, tossing it into the trunk. As he did, the bag ripped and split wide open. Newspapers spilled out. The dog barked. The old woman hushed him, pulling him away. And there, on the ground, among all the dead bodies, was the Ziploc bag. He'd forgotten all about it. The earrings. His father. The plain white envelope. Inside the envelope, there was a handwritten letter:

To my son, Theodore,

Last night I had a dream that wasn't a dream. I know it was real. I was surrounded by people. So many people. We were drifting through the clouds. All of us together, and it felt so warm. I felt so happy and at peace. And there was singing. Beautiful music. I don't know how I knew the words, but they touched me, and I was singing too. I didn't want to leave, but I thought I

*should come back and tell you not to worry about me. I
will be okay. I am going where I want to be.*

With love,
Your mother

P.S. Your father wasn't there, but I'll find him.

It wasn't his mother's handwriting. It wasn't her
voice either. Teddy folded the letter up and put it in his
pocket. Maybe there was another patient with a son
named Theodore.

"Maybe it was aliens," said the girl buying the Modest
Mouse album.

"I heard it was the government," said her friend.
"*Our* government."

"No way!" said the Modest Mouse girl. "That's
fucking bullshit."

"That's seven dollars and ninety-eight cents," said
Teddy.

"I know," said her friend. "But that's what
everyone's saying."

"What the fuck would they do that for?" said the
Modest Mouse girl.

"Seven dollars and ninety-eight cents," said Teddy.

The Modest Mouse girl handed him a ten-dollar
bill.

"Yeah well, like, they knew it was going to happen
and shit," said her friend. "And they just, like, let it
happen."

"But why?"

"So we could go to war. With Iraq."

"What? I thought it was Iran."

"Actually," said Teddy, "it's Afghanistan."

"What?"

"Whatever."

"That's so fucked up."

"Have a nice day," said Teddy.

"We're not safe anymore," said Marco, Teddy's assistant and only remaining employee. Marco was a college dropout. He was twenty-eight and still lived like a student, which was poorly and with his direction on hold. "That's what it is. That's why everyone's freaking out. We thought no one would do that shit to us. And then they fucking did."

"Your till is two dollars short," said Teddy.

"This is what we get for sticking our nose in other people's business," said Marco.

"Why is your till two dollars short?"

"This must be how Darth Vader felt when the Rebel Alliance attacked the Death Star."

"Just give me two dollars, Marco."

Teddy was considering selling the shop. Marco was interested in buying it, but he had bad credit and no collateral. No one else was interested. The shop was one of the few spaces still open in a decrepit strip mall in a jagged part of town. Its roughness had once been part of its charm. But its time was coming to an end. Teddy was ready to let go.

"What'll ya do if you close it down?" said Marco.

"Move to Cuba. Get drunk. Write a book."

"Big dreams," said Marco. "I didn't know you could write."

"I can't," said Teddy. "But all you need is a good story."

"Have you got one?"

"No," said Teddy. "Not yet."

"Maybe you'll get one in Cuba."

Teddy didn't go to Cuba. He went back to the diner and waited for Janine to come in for her usual coffee to go. She wasn't surprised to see him. It was a perfectly normal thing to do, to be in the same place you'd been in before. Most people did it. It was called "habit". Teddy had developed one in the course of the grieving process. Bumping into Janine again was only a matter of time. It was pure coincidence. It was a sign.

"A sign of?" said Janine.

Teddy laughed. "Gosh. I don't know. You drink too much coffee?"

"I do," she said.

Teddy pulled his mother's letter out of his pocket. It had torn in two places. There was a smudge of something purple on one of its edges. "Do you know what this is?" he said. He opened it. He held onto it while Janine leaned in closer to inspect it. Janine with the freckle on her right ear.

"I do," she said. "Yes. It's a letter from your mother."

"Do you know who wrote it?"

"I did," she said. "Your mother dictated it to me. She asked me to not give it to you until she was gone. I liked the bit about the singing." She blew into her coffee. Steam whirled around in the chilly air between them. "I'm sorry," she said. "I sound like I'm writing a review." She made a funny face. He'd never seen her be this easy, so real.

"Thing is," he said, "I'm not sure what to make of this. I mean, I can't imagine my mother singing."

"How many times have you read it?"

"Double digits. Been trying to decipher it with my decoder ring. I'd left it on the nightstand one night and woke up with it in my hands. I'm sure most people would take that as some sort of a sign."

Most people take everything as a sign, Janine told him. A dog barking could mean don't sell the house, a broken vase is remember to water the garden, a song on the car radio says, "*Centuries are what it meant to me*," but it was really saying, "Don't forget me." Teddy hadn't expected signs. He'd expected nothing. This was his mother they were talking about.

"People need signs," said Janine. "It's natural. It's normal. It's okay."

"But this is nothing like the woman I knew," said Teddy. "For one thing, she wasn't in the least bit spiritual. And she didn't like crowds. Or clouds, for that matter. What was in those drips anyway?"

"At this point, it's all about keeping her comfortable," Janine had said to him that day she'd stuck the tube into his mother's arm, her useless, burdensome body becoming a twisted knot. "It's just the shock of the morphine," Janine had said to him. From that moment on, Teddy's mother never looked anything even close to comfortable again.

"I know you were just doing your job," he said to Janine now, letter in hand, mother in the ground. "But I find this all rather odd."

"I know," said Janine. "You want answers. I know. Clarity comes with time. It does." She put her hand on his arm. It was warm from the coffee cup. Or it was just warm from being alive.

"Is that what the good book says?" said Teddy.

"Sure is."

"Well, that's good to know."

"Glad I could help," she said. Her red lips smiled. The tears were gone.

"I'll let you get back to it, then," he said. "Your job."

"It was nice seeing you again," she said. "Maybe I'll see you again next time you find yourself on this side of town, absent-mindedly working up an appetite."

"What can I say?" he said. "I thought this was my sign."

"You know," she said, "I can think of much better places to eat."

"Really?"

"Oh, yes."

"Well look," he said, "maybe if, say next time I find myself on this side of town, you know, maybe you could let me know about one of those places. I mean, if you think that would be okay? I mean. You know. You know what I mean?"

"I think so," she said.

"Okay. So. Maybe see you then?"

"Maybe."

He'd waited for three hours. He'd sat in his car with David Bowie and a tuna fish sandwich. He would have stayed until ten, but he didn't trust Marco enough to lock up the store. Maybe she was tied up. Maybe she'd thought he'd meant the next Friday. Or maybe when she said "maybe" she meant maybe and nothing else.

"*We can be heroes*," Bowie sang as Teddy sat in his car in the diner parking lot a week later. "*Just for one day.*" He saw Janine walking towards the diner. Janine and her red lips and that nurse who always made him feel like a creep. He waited for them to come back out. He stopped them as they approached the hospital entrance.

"Miss me?" he said.

"We don't have time for this," the other nurse said.

"It's okay," Janine said. "I'll catch up."

"You were going to tell me about those other places to eat," Teddy said.

Janine looked at her watch.

"You're in a hurry," he said.

"Kind of," she said.

"Maybe next time," he said. "Or I can just keep on eating in that shithole until you agree to spend some time with me."

She gave him a few minutes to consider what he'd just said, to really come to grips with the magnitude of the biting atmosphere he'd created with those words, to remember how nurses do that thing they do, to wait for her to offer him some words.

"Hey, you know what?" she said. "I'd be lying if I

said I didn't want to talk to you about something."

"Ah, see, I told you it was a sign."

"But I do need to maintain some degree of professionalism."

He could remind her that his mother was dead now, that he didn't care about her profession. "Of course," said Teddy. "It's a bit chilly. Shall we?"

"No, no," said Janine. "I really am in a hurry."

"Right," said Teddy.

"So this... situation. Whatever you might think it is. It's not."

The tip of her nose had gone as red as her lips from the cold. Teddy was on fire.

"I'm really sorry," she said. "I did realize last time we met. I should have said something. And I'm sorry if I've done anything in any way to lead you on or to make you think — shit, sorry, that's my pager. I do need to get back. But I do want to say, I am truly sorry for your loss, but maybe it might make you feel better if I told you how deeply your mother's death affected me."

"*My* mother?"

"Yes. It has something to do with, well, all those people dying like that. And that letter she had me transcribe for you, and just the way she was, the look on her face when she passed. It gave me consolation I didn't even know I'd needed. And I know that sounds bizarre and out of context and absolutely, and believe me, I know, inappropriate and insensitive to you, but at that point in time, I'd needed that. Your mother's passing. I needed to see it. To see that it is okay. For someone like her."

"You mean because she was... what?"

"You'd said it yourself — she wasn't a spiritual woman."

Teddy smiled. He had no words.

"You know," she said, "sometimes, when people are grieving, they attach themselves to things. And sometimes it's the wrong things."

She didn't say much more than that, just goodbye and good luck and thanks for bringing your mother into my hospital to die. That was the end of it.

Teddy drove over the bridge one last time. He parked in front of his mother's old apartment. Someone else's mother was living in it now, but it still looked the same. Then he stopped by the cemetery. The mother he knew wouldn't mind that he'd never come back here to see her.

On his way home, Teddy stopped on the Verrazano. He let his engine run, hazards flashing, and kept his radio on. He got out of his car and looked down over the bridge into the darkness of the water that drifted beneath him. People passing by honked their horns and shouted. He would find out eventually, wouldn't he? He'd know if his mother was really singing. He closed his eyes and tried to imagine it, and he wondered if he would see it too.

CHILDREN WHO SCREAM

But I'm only in the outskirts and in the fringes,
On the edge and off the avenue.
~ Suzanne Vega
"Left of Center"

Charlie drove slowly up East Capitol, the road a wide line of blue pointing at the big white dome ahead of her. Thick, leafy trees stood up straight on the red brick pavement lining both sides of the road, perfectly placed and planted according to some astute plan. Structured symmetry. Deviant nature. A few of them had grown taller than the white buildings that hid behind them. She searched for an empty spot, a space not already filled with a neutral-colored car. People walking along the sidewalk were neutral too. Browns, grays and blues. Nothing purple or hot pink. No neon green, and no place to park. She'd be late, as per usual. The same old Charlie.

As soon as she put the car into park, a text message arrived telling her that they had to leave the museum and were now at a McDonald's about a mile away. Charlie hesitated. She looked at her reflection in the window of her Prius. *Not* the same old Charlie. She began the long

84

walk to the golden arches.

Capitol Hill isn't really much of a hill, but Charlie had once thought of it as an impossible mountain. That was before she'd met Bill, before he'd asked her to consider a life of lecture halls and cherry blossom festivals, before she knew of the convenience of maids and dog walkers, before she knew anything better than the intellectually bone-dry swamps of rural Georgia. She'd said yes for two reasons: she loved him, and she was ready to go. But she'd already, on her own, become equipped with enough intellectual gear to tackle that mountain. She was smart and driven, very uncommon in her dinky little hometown. Even Savannah, with its clever houses and co-ed population, was not much more than a hot, dirty fish tank. When they left, she said farewell to Georgia and swore she'd never see anything in it ever again. That was almost sixteen years ago. Two weeks ago, Charlie got a phone call. Georgia had found her.

Through the window, she could see the halter-top and the two-month-old perm with cheap highlights of her baby sister, Angie, who was inattentively dipping French fries into a thick pool of ketchup floating in a yellow burger wrapper. Sitting across from Angie were the wide shoulders of her husband, Trey. Another figure, a frail, defeated form that seemed to be sinking into her seat, was beside him, lost in his shadow. It was Sara, the niece Charlie had known only as a baby. The new baby, Jacob, the "happy surprise" she'd heard all about, had been parked crookedly into a wooden highchair at the end of the table, where he sat anxiously chewing on his

Happy Meal box.

"There's Auntie Charlotte!" Angie shouted with an arm waving in the air as Charlie approached them. "Late as usual," she said, grinning. "Say hello to Auntie Charlotte, Jacob." The child dribbled out some cardboard.

"Hello, Jacob," said Charlie. "So nice to finally meet you." She reached her hand over to greet her brother-in-law. "Trey," she said.

"Charlie," he nodded. He let go of her hand, grabbed a fistful of fries, and dipped them into Angie's ketchup.

"We had a little incident at the museum," said Angie. She wiggled over to make room on the bench for Charlie. "You hungry? I've still got some fries and half a cheeseburger."

"No, thanks," said Charlie. She sat down next to her sister and across from her niece. Sara was a long, thin thing with a long, pale face, chemically black hair (Charlie had always known her as a redhead) and dark, oversized clothing. There was an apple cupped in her hands. A flock of chicken nuggets sat neglected on the table in front of her.

"Sara," Angie snipped. "Say hello to your Aunt Charlotte."

Sara cleared her throat and said, "Hi," her voice squashed like a mouse under an elephant.

"Gosh, look at you," said Charlie. "You must have been about three or four the last time I saw you. How old are you now?"

Sara cleared her throat again. "Eighteen," she said,

hiding her lips with a boney, white hand. Sitting beside her beefy father, the girl was a bleak silhouette, a ghost of something. Charlie didn't know what. There was very little of Trey in her stiff and timid ill-at-ease. Trey was, and always had been, more like a rowdy orangutan. He had dark beady eyes and a thick reddish beard and mustache. Charlie knew what little he hid beneath the tattered baseball hat.

"Do I look like the mother of an eighteen-year-old?" said Angie. She tugged at her halter-top and brushed the frizzy ends of her hair away from her neck. "I can hardly believe it sometimes."

"She's starting college in the fall," said Trey. "My baby rodent's almost all grown up." He punched her lightly on the arm.

"Tell Auntie Charlotte what you wanted to major in," said Angie. "She wanted to do art, just like you did, Charlie. Even Daddy says how much she reminds him of you when you was young."

"She ain't like either one of us," said Trey, putting his arm around her. "But we like her anyways." He pulled her towards him, bending her upper half, her lower half still rooted firmly on the bench. Her arms were pulled in tightly to her sides, as if glued to her difficult torso. She was wearing a long-sleeved shirt, and her fingers grabbed at the sleeves, holding them up over her wrists, hiding as much of her as they possibly could. She gave a slight, uncomfortable smile. Trey's arm let go, and the girl sprang back upright.

"Ain't that exactly what Daddy used to say about you, Charlie?" Angie said. "She ain't like any of us.

Sara, sweetheart, you'll be pleased to know that your Auntie Charlotte was even more unpopular in school than you. But I still think it was due to that time you let that Melissa skank beat you up. What was that all about?"

"I can't remember," said Charlie.

"Hey, remember Adrian?" said Angie. "You were so in love with him."

"I don't know if I'd call it love," said Charlie.

"Remember the time he took you on that date," Angie said with four fingers clawing in the air around the outlandish idea of Charlie's romantic life. "He was like, what, six, seven years older than you and pretty much engaged to his girlfriend at the time and Mamma warned you not to get too interested cause he was only sparing your feelings by taking you to Great Skates on your birthday. Everybody knew how much you were in love with him. You even swore on Grandpap's grave that you were going to marry him one day."

"Did I?" said Charlie.

"Didn't he even buy you some cheap, plastic bracelet out of a vending machine?"

"It was metal," said Charlie.

"You cried for weeks over him. I always think about that whenever I hear that "Total Eclipse of the Heart" song. You must have played that record trillions of times. Lord, how I hated that stupid song. Everyone did. Over and over and over..."

"Turn around, bright eyes," Trey sang like a fat woman on the verge of a great, overly-theatric operatic death.

"Like, how did you not get sick of that?" said Angie. "Gosh, we all sure did. Don't you remember?"

"Speaking of Daddy," Charlie said, "how is he?"

"Oh, you know Daddy. Same old, same old. Bandit died a few months ago. Got run over by a car. Hit him pretty bad. You know how much he loved Bandit."

"Bandit?" said Charlie. "I thought he died years ago."

"How's that blue-balls husband of yours?" said Trey.

"Don't you be starting that up again," said Angie.

"Charlie knows I'm only kidding. I'm just giving her shit. It's what I do."

"Bill's fine," said Charlie. "He's up for tenure, so it's been tense lately. In a good way. He was hoping you'd change your minds and stay with us for a couple of days. He hates thinking of you spending so much on a hotel."

"That's real sweet of him," said Angie. "But you know."

"Tell Bill thanks for the thought," said Trey, "but I can't be seen taking hospitality from traitors."

"Oh, hush up, Trey," said Angie. "I said don't start."

"I'm not starting nothing."

Angie rolled her eyes.

"What? What did I start?" said Trey. "Huh? Tell, me, Ang. What did I start? I'm only saying we don't need to be staying at theirs. That's it."

Jacob stirred in his highchair and began to cry.

"Now look what you done," said Angie. She

grabbed one of Jacob's feet and shook it gently. "Momma wasn't yelling at you, Jay-Jay. Look! Look what Momma has." She dangled a wimpy French fry in the air. This made Jacob cry harder. He became angry, resentful. His high-pitched cries became deep, throaty wails. "This here is why we had to leave the museum," Angie said. "He's been fussing all morning. Let's just eat our fries now, Jacob. Momma doesn't want one of them children who scream all the time."

"Jacob!" Trey shouted. "Do what your momma says. Daddy paid good money for them fries."

Angie dipped the French fry into her ketchup and rubbed some of it on the boy's lips. He clamped them shut as tight as he could. He kicked furiously at his mother's arms. "Eat, Jacob," she said. The boy refused. He used his hands, two plump, dirty mitts, to bat his mother's offering away. "Honestly," she said, "I don't know what to do with you."

"Maybe he isn't hungry," said Sara.

"Give momma a break, Jacob," Angie pleaded.

"Boy," said Trey, "if you don't quit your fussing, your dairy air's gonna meet a big can of whoop-ass."

Angie rolled her eyes again.

"What?" said Trey.

"You and your 'Look what a big, bad redneck I am' thing," said Angie.

"Maybe he's sick or something," Sara said.

Angie dropped the French fry on Jacob's tray and unlatched it. She picked him up and held him. He hid his face in her chest, his cries muffled by her body, as she rubbed the back of his head. "I don't know what's wrong with him today," she said. "He ain't usually like this. You can tell by how chunky he is he's usually a good eater."

"All I meant anyways," said Trey, "is Bill and I don't see eye to eye about most things. Charlie knows that."

"Oh for Pete's sake, Trey," said Angie. "Are you still on that?"

"So, Sara," said Charlie, "what school are you going to?"

Sara looked at her quickly and then averted her eyes to look down at the apple in her hands. She'd only taken two bites. "Gainesville," she said.

"Guess who we saw this morning, Charlie?" said Trey. "We sorta got to see him. Didn't we, Ang?"

Jacob had some of Angie's hair in one of his hands. He was silent and still. Angie looked at his face to see if he was asleep before she said, "That wasn't him," in a hushed voice. "We were too far away anyways."

"You know, he does kind of look like Bill," Trey said.

"No, he doesn't," said Angie.

"They all look a lot alike," said Trey.

"I think it was only a decoy or some other important person," said Angie. "He was too small-looking to be him."

"That's what you'd said about Stephen King too," said Trey. "But that was him."

"Why would Stephen King be at Disney World?" said Angie, forgetting to use her quiet voice. Jacob twitched and pulled on her hair. "Ow, baby. Let go of

Momma's hair."

"Same as everybody else," said Trey. "Space Mountain is a universal joy, Ang. I've told you that a billion times."

Angie was trying to release Jacob's hold of her loose curls, but he resisted. The more she worked at it, the tighter the boy gripped, until he began to cry again.

"Everyone who's anyone has had their butt in those seats," Trey said. "You don't know whose dairy air was in there before yours. Maybe Tom Cruise or maybe some jerk you work with. Who knows?"

"Hush, baby boy," Angie said.

"I even saw a sniper up on the roof," said Trey. "You know, to protect his ass from terrorists and negro-haters."

"That's not what they call 'em anymore, Trey," said Angie. She reached a hand into a diaper bag on the table and pulled out a teething ring. She tried putting it into the boy's mouth, but he batted it away. "Almost forgot to tell you, Charlie — do you remember Dan? You know, the preacher at Emmanuel I told you about. Well, he's got a new book out. It's a good one. It made me laugh and cry and praise the Lord all at the same time. And I thought, Charlie should read this."

"Dan?" Charlie said. "Not sure it rings any bells."

"Anyways, I had you a copy, but Trey gave it to some homeless man outside our hotel."

"He said he was hungry, so I fed him," said Trey.

"He was looking for a sandwich, Trey. Not something to read."

"I gave him a Jesus sandwich. They ought to gather

up all those lazy bums, make them enlist. Put them to some use. It's disturbing seeing them all rolled up on the sidewalk like that. And we've got a whole fuckload of criminals overcrowding the prisons on my dollar we could use for the first battalion. Even Bill couldn't argue the logic in that."

"Oh, stop being so ridiculous," said Angie. "Keep your opinions to yourself for once. Please."

"I don't have opinions. I have facts. You see this scar on my arm?" He pushed the sleeve of his shirt up and threw his fat, hairy arm at Charlie. "You see that? What's that? That's a fact."

"Nobody wants to be seeing your scar all the time," Angie said, serving up yet another eye roll to go with it.

"I'll bet old Bill wouldn't like to see it, that's for one," Trey said. He smirked and gave Charlie a wink.

"Can we just not talk about it anymore, please?" Angie said.

Jacob spat up a thick white liquid that slid down his chin. Angie wiped it up with her napkin. "Anyhow," she said, "I'll order another one and have it shipped to you. Dan's a real good writer. I think you'll appreciate what he says in his book."

Trey tapped on Sara's arm. "Lemme out. I need another cheeseburger." Sara stood up shyly to make way for her father. He was a giant lumber of a man, but somehow, Charlie had remembered him as being much smaller. "You need some soda, Sulky Sara?" he said.

Sara shook her head and slunk back into her seat.

"Get some fresh milk for Jacob," said Angie.

Trey bouldered off, and the tension that had

mounted on the table loosened. Sara's blackness was even more gauche now against the kitschy orange background. Angie poked at Charlie's leg under the table. She leaned over and whispered, "It's the meds."

Sara looked down at her hands, which were resting on the edge of the table, clasped tightly together, one thumb caressing the other.

Angie poked Charlie again. "She don't know I told you about it," she said in the vicinity of Charlie's ear.

Sara cleared her throat with a polite nudge. She folded up all the used and dirty wrappers, napkins and ketchup packets. She flattened the empty French fry and hot apple pie holders. She reconstructed Jacob's demolished Happy Meal box, and she placed everything neatly inside, closing over the mangled flaps on the top to conceal the mess inside, and she sat the box proudly in the center of the highchair tray.

Angie rolled her eyes. "Thank you, Miss Sara," she said.

"I don't know if your mom told you this," Charlie said, "but I went to Gainesville for a year before I transferred over to Savannah."

"She wants to go to Savannah," said Angie, "but Trey wants her to stay close to home for the first two years. Maybe get her associate's first and then see. He's hoping she'll get married so he won't need to be worrying about her forever."

"Let her husband pay for it," said Trey. He had a double cheeseburger, two large sodas and a small cup of milk in his hands. "If she wants to keep going after two years. I don't mind giving her a little bit of something, but I don't earn enough to be sending her to some pricey art school." He held out the drinks for Angie and Sara to take from him and tossed the cheeseburger onto the table. He slammed his hands on the table and pulled his way into his seat, opened his wrapper, and shoved half a cheeseburger into his mouth.

"What about a Pell Grant?" Charlie said. "Doesn't she qualify? Or scholarships. Student loans."

"Our finances are none of your beeswax," said Trey.

"Trey says we don't need no more debt," said Angie.

"Okay," said Charlie. "That's cool. But have you at least taken her to any of the Smithsonian museums?"

"We were at the one with the dinosaurs this morning," Angie said. "Before Jacob starting kicking and fussing. I wanted us to go to that Holocaust museum, but Trey says it's a bad idea. I'd cry too much, and he don't want his kids to see all them boney dead bodies."

"The only thing they need to know about the Holocaust is the end, when our boys come in and save the day," said Trey. He laughed. Charlie wanted to kick him in the face. "The Christians liberating the Jews. They still owe us big time for that."

"Stop trying to be funny, Trey," Angie said. "That's very disrespectful."

"I think Sara might be interested in seeing some of the art museums," Charlie said. "The National Portrait Gallery has some fantastic collections. The Sackler and Freer galleries are great, too. Do you like Asian art,

Sara?"

Sara pulled her arms into her flat chest as if she was hugging something. She smiled and shook her head. Her long sleeve had shortened just enough for Charlie to spy several little lines, some of them still cherry fresh, and some the matured brown wounds of days not buried deep enough yet in the past.

"She's real into that Japanimotion stuff," said Trey.

"Anime," said Sara. She was looking at Charlie now, really seeing her, for the first time since she'd arrived. There was a little light in her eyes. "And Manga."

Jacob's cries started up again. Angie propped him up on the table. "Who's my little man?" she said. Then she bounced him up and down like a ball. An elderly couple sitting at the table next to theirs were watching them. They were saying things no one could hear over Jacob's cries.

"Give him here," said Trey, reaching over to stick his big hands under the child's pudgy arms. "He usually listens to his daddy." Trey hoisted his son up and down like a toy. "Woo...wee...," he said with every bump on the child's pampered bottom. Jacob's cries deepened. Something about them was disturbing, but Charlie preferred to think it was only her inexperience with children that made her uncomfortable.

Trey finally gave up the game and held the boy agreeably in his lap. "Hey Ang," he said, placing a hand on the boy's face. "He's burning up."

"I did think he was a little warm," she said.

"He's damn near on fire!" said Trey.

"I was thinking maybe it was due to it's so hot outside," said Angie.

"We've been sitting in an icebox for nearly an hour, and you think he's just hot cause it's hot outside?" He handed the boy over to his mother, a discarded package of unsatisfying goods. "Do you see now how dumb your sister is, Charlie?"

"That's what I thought," said Angie. "It's the heat. I guess I wasn't really thinking."

"No, you really wasn't thinking," Trey said. "I swear sometimes you've got jellybeans for brains."

"That's why I took his socks off," Angie said. "Try and cool him down a bit. It's so hot here. Muggy. Not like it is at home."

Trey tapped on Sara's arm. "Up. We're fixing to go."

"Go where?" said Angie.

"Back to the room so your son can be put down," he said.

They all quickly unsettled themselves. A heavily soiled baby buggy containing the dismembered bodies of once-soggy animal crackers materialized from thin air, and the family bond Charlie had hoped to rekindle got thrown into the trash with Jacob's Happy Meal prize. "Sara can stay with me," she said quickly. "I can take her to the galleries. If that's okay with you and Trey. I'd really like to spend some time with my niece."

"Oh," said Angie. "Um, I don't know. Trey, what do you think?"

"Yeah, fine with me," said Trey.

"Would you like to go with Auntie Charlotte,

Sara?" Angie said. "It's okay if you'd rather stay with us." She gave Trey a look. Charlie always hated that look.

When they stepped outside, they met with a hard wall of heat and humidity. Trey tugged Sara's sleeves up. "You're gonna boil up in there, rat girl," he said. "Sara soup."

"I'm fine," Sara said, tugging herself away from him.

Angie pulled Charlie back inside. "Call us if anything happens," she said. "She can be a little weird because of her meds."

"It'll be fine," said Charlie. "I can handle a little weird."

On the way to the museum, Charlie stopped at a street vendor and bought two bottles of cold water.

"No, thank you," said Sara.

"Please," said Charlie. "Your mother will kill me if I let you dehydrate."

Sara took a small sip. She held the sweating bottle in her hands the rest of the way. It was still full by the time they reached the gallery, and Charlie had to throw it away. No liquids of any kind could enter the building, a precaution meant more for the safety of the museum's guests than its priceless inhabitants.

Sara told Charlie she knew a little about the gallery, that she'd wanted to visit it, but she was afraid to ask her parents. They would only say "no".

"They're not like us," said Charlie with a smile.

Sara walked through the gallery like a robot with stiff, rigid arms occasionally popping up to point at something. Her elbows stuck to her sides, but her face had seemed to change completely. It softened, became full of genuine expression, of life. She spoke in rapid beats, telling Charlie all about the history of Manga. "You can see the influence of Western culture in the eyes," she said.

"You're right," said Charlie. "You really can."

"Yeah," said Sara. "They're called dot eyes."

"How do you know so much about this?"

"A boy I used to be friends with told me a lot. But I mostly read about it on the Internet."

Charlie remembered that one aspect of Sara's so-called "condition" was her excessive time spent online, not interacting with her family, which her doctor felt was leading her deeper into her depression and antisocial tendencies. They'd had to put a strict curfew on her computer time, only allowing her one hour a day, two if she needed it for schoolwork. She'd been cutting herself, mostly her arms, but sometimes her thighs as well, since Jacob's arrival. When Angie phoned Charlie to announce their big, upcoming vacation plans, she'd said it had always been just normal teenage stuff Sara was going through, but it had gotten a lot worse. She only had a few friends, who were "kinda Donnie Darko". In Charlie's day, it was Siouxsie and the Banshees and Edgar Allen Poe, freaks finding freaks. With Charlie, it was just a phase. Charlie also remembered that Sara going to Gainesville was contingent on her behavior over the summer break. Until they'd entered the museum, there was little to break Charlie's opinion that Sara had become too inhibited to exhibit any kind of behavior.

"Do you know Tin Tin?" said Sara.

"Tin Tin?" said Charlie.

"Yeah, do you know about Tin Tin?"

"Only a little. He's a cartoon, right?"

"A French cartoon. Some people say there's an American influence in Maga, and others think it's more European. Like Tin Tin."

"And what do you say?"

Sara scrunched up her face as she thought about it. "I think it is more American," she said. "American culture pervades everything."

"But not any of this?" said Charlie.

"No way," said Sara. "This stuff is really... I dunno. Different. Really stiff. Manga's more animated."

"Now that's interesting," said Charlie. "The evolution of Japanese art. That could be a great thing to study. From the aesthetic to the agile."

"Or death to life," said Sara.

"Boring to fun."

"Poised to prompt."

Charlie felt a chill, the nervous excitement of climbing mountains.

"I wish I could do this kind of stuff," said Sara.

"Do you draw?" said Charlie.

"I'm not very good."

"I'd love to see some of your work."

Sara slid a hand into a pocket somewhere beneath her billowy black guise and produced a small square of folded-up drafting paper. She'd drawn it, she said, on the drive up from Georgia. Charlie unfolded it and found a little Japanese girl the color of ash looking up at her, pools of crimson tears in a set of large, almond eyes. Behind her was an idiosyncratic mushroom explosion. The words "I died because of the beliefs of my government" fell in a spiral out of the girl's frowning mouth.

"Wow," said Charlie. "Would you mind — could I keep this?"

Sara smiled.

"I'm just so impressed by how much you know, your interest and passion," said Charlie. "That's what makes great teachers, if not great artists."

"Do you still teach, Aunt Charlie? Momma said you taught at a big school up here."

"Not so much. I'm adjunct now. I mostly do research for friends who write books. But it's all boring stuff. Bill's the teacher."

"Does he teach Art History too?"

"Economics, if you can believe that. We have very little in common in that regard. He took to it much better than I did. I preferred being a student, sitting in a quiet room with my books and my thoughts. Bill likes to talk. He's good with people. Me, not so much."

"I know. Momma says you were always fighting with Grandpap."

"Well, it takes two to tango," said Charlie.

She let Sara wander through the gallery on her own while she went outside to phone Bill. "I think she's just in the wrong place," she said. "I know this. I was there."

"It's not your job to save her, Charlie," Bill said. "You can't do it." Though he was sympathetic, he felt it was possible that some of Charlie's ideas were a matter of transference, and not necessarily either relative or curative.

"I just want to take her home," she said. "Make her happy. Get her off those pills at least."

"She's not yours, Charlie. And, most importantly, she's not you. Who are you really trying to save? Stay out of it. Keep away. You're long gone, remember?"

Charlie knew she would never forgive herself for not trying to help Sara in some way, but other than kidnapping, no sure solution came to mind.

Back at the hotel, Jacob had been given a cool bath and some baby aspirin. Trey was watching the Braves game with the sound muted.

"I saved you some of my chow mein, Sara sweetie," Angie said.

Sara went into the bathroom to wash her hands.

"Remember not to lock the door," Angie said.

"I know."

"How was she?" Angie asked Charlie as soon as the door was shut. "Did she get weird on ya at all? I apologize if she did."

"No," said Charlie. "She wasn't weird at all. She was fine. She was great, in fact. That girl really knows her stuff. We had a really nice time."

"I meant, how was she behaving?" Angie said. "Was she okay or what?"

"She was happy," Charlie said. "Is that what you mean?"

"Thanks for babysitting the rodent, Charlie," said

Trey.

"Actually," said Charlie, "I was going to say... I've been thinking that, if you'd like, we can let her come up and spend a week or two with us before she starts school. It would be a great way for her to adjust to being away from home."

"I don't know about that," Angie said.

"She's not so good with strangers," Trey said.

"Charlie's strange, but I wouldn't call her a stranger," Angie said.

"She's kin," Trey said. "But that don't mean she's kind." He smirked playfully at Charlie.

The toilet flushed.

"Come on out now, Sara sweetie," Angie said.

"But, truthfully, Charlie girl," Trey said, "I'd rather not expose my kid to Bill's liberalities. And that's the long and short of it."

"Charlie wasn't asking you, Trey," Angie said. She knocked lightly on the bathroom door. "Sara, sweetie. Come on now."

"I'm her daddy," Trey said. "She needs to be asking me."

The baby began to whimper.

"Bill ain't a Christian, for one thing," Trey said. "And he don't know much about the real world. That's my main issue right there."

"What's that got to do with anything?" Angie said. "You even said so yourself, Bill's a real nice person. Charlie just wants to spend some time with her niece, is all."

"She just did spend some time with her," Trey said.

"You're just being stubborn now," Angie said. "Just like Daddy."

Jacob let out a little cry. Angie picked him up immediately.

"I said no, and that's the end of it."

"Never mind," said Charlie. "It was just a thought."

Angie rolled her eyes at Charlie and mouthed, "Just like Daddy."

"Go! Go! Go, you pussy!" Trey shouted at the television.

Jacob screamed.

"Dammit, Trey," Angie said.

"I should go," said Charlie.

"He's hot again," Angie said.

"Take him out!" Trey shouted at the television.

Charlie hugged Angie and Jacob together. She could feel the child's fever on her cheek. "Let's try to do better about keeping in touch, Ang," she said.

"I know what you think of me," Trey said.

Angie rolled her eyes again. She took Jacob over to the window where the air conditioner was blowing full blast against the curtains.

"I don't know what you mean," Charlie said.

Angie stuck her fingers through the curtains and looked out.

"Yes, you do," Trey said.

"Sara sweetie," Angie shouted. She was still looking out the window. "Come on out now. You hear me?"

"I love my family," said Trey.

"I never said you didn't," said Charlie. "But Sara's

my family too. I wouldn't mind getting to know her a little better."

"Your family, eh?" Trey said. "Charlie's family. All them stupid ignorant folks she left back in the sticks. That the family you're talking about?"

"Sara? Answer me, sweetie," Angie shouted.

"Who do you think of as your 'family', Charlie?" Trey said. "Tell me."

"What have I ever done to you?" Charlie said. "Why have you always tried to instigate something with me? And with Bill! You waste so much time putting things into these silly little boxes. It's always "we" and "us" against "you" and "them". What a small, little world you live in, Trey. You seem to have such a problem with the fact that I have evolved."

"Yes, you have," Trey said. "Grown right out of your skin."

"I've grown out of my skin. So what? A skin that, I have to tell you, never fit me. Ever. Never, in my fucking life."

"Charlie!" said Angie.

"Sorry, Ang. I just... I'm really sorry. It was so stupid of me to think things would be different, but we're separate for a reason. And the truth is, I'm okay with that. It's better this way."

"We're not the ones ashamed of where we come from," Trey said. "That's your problem."

"Fuck off, Trey!" Charlie said.

Angie rolled her eyes. "Same old Charlie," she said.

"Really, Ang? Really?" Charlie said. "After all these years, you still haven't figured it out? Gee, sis, you really are stupid."

"Hey!" Trey shouted.

Angie turned and looked vacantly out the window, the baby Jacob either dead or sleeping in her bosom.

"Thank you," Charlie said.

Trey laughed. "What the hell for?" he said.

But Charlie said nothing. She just glared at him, smiling.

"Sara!" Angie screamed. "Out! Now!"

Jacob cried. Angie took him over to the bed and sat down. "Mommy didn't mean to scare you, baby boy," she said.

Trey brought his attention back to the television, but the game was over.

Charlie knocked on the bathroom door. "Sara. I'm leaving now. I just wanted to say goodbye. It was so nice spending time with you today."

"Bye," said a small voice through the door. Then came the slight sound of the lock clicking slowly. Charlie reached for the handle, but she didn't grab it. She could hear Bill's voice in her head, admonishing her in his kind, caring way, telling her she ought to just leave it alone. For her own good, he was telling her. Walk away. Be long gone.

"Worst play in history," Trey said to the television.

"Who's Momma's little angel?" Angie said to Jacob.

"Well, it's been a blast, kids," Charlie said to the room as she opened the door to leave. "Y'all come back now, ya hear?"

And then she was gone. Long gone.

DECORATIONS OF RED

'Cause nothing lasts forever,
But I will always love you.
~ Neko Case
"Don't Forget Me"

Jesse looks out of his front bay window and sees white. White houses, white trees, white trash cans. It must have snowed all night. He looks over the white plane that was once his suburban victory garden and shakes his head. He watches a flat metal flag of defeat rise and fall behind the mound of white that hides the candy apple red Camaro across the street. Jesse had told him not to park in the fucking road. Except for the tracks Sonny has made to his car and the piles he has dug up around it, the whole street is pristine. A street of hidden dirt. Jesse sips his coffee and turns on the TV. There's not a chance in hell that anything is open, but he checks. The names of schools scroll alphabetically along the bottom of the screen as the weatherman points to swirling waves of white across the entire Tri-State area. He can hear the alarm radio switch on upstairs. *Gone away is the bluebird, here to stay is a new bird...*

"Go back to bed," he says to the sleepy figure

making its way down the stairs. But she is silent. She has her robe on, untied, and her knees peek out from under his old Steelers jersey. She is cold. The figure turns back and disappears. She is gone.

He sees her again, coming from the kitchen, in her pink robe and her fuzzy slippers, ponytail in her hair. "How much did we get?" she asks. She is looking out the bay window. It only takes two inches to close the schools out here. She could be worried about having to rearrange lesson plans, but she wouldn't feel sorry for the kids. These days are really for them.

"No parent in their right mind would put a kid on a bus in this," Jesse says. "But I checked. Everything's shut. Even the city. Poor Jersey's gonna have to stay in Jersey today."

"Ain't that a shame," she snickers. She ties her robe and heads for the kitchen. She does not float, as he'd always expected. She almost jiggles. She is full of joy. "Do you want pancakes?" she calls back to him. He peers out the window again and sees Sonny digging around his front tires with his gloved hands. He's cleared off the hood, its panel of cherry red a sign of life to planes passing over. By the time he gets that thing freed, they'll be back down the street with the plow. Besides, where's he gonna put it? He can't drive it. He hasn't even cleared off the driveway yet.

"Hey ho," says Stacy from the kitchen doorway, "I asked if you want pancakes."

He hadn't ignored her. He'd tried to, but it never worked.

"Nah," he says, "I'd better do some shoveling.

Supposed to start up again in a few hours." He sorts through the mess in the hall closet and pulls out his boots. "Need to get cracking."

When they first bought this house, Jesse's father came out from the city for a weekend and complained the whole time. The water tasted funny, the pizza was like rubbery shit, and it took forever just to go out for a loaf of bread or a melon, even though he's never seen his father eat any kind of melon.

"Why do you gotta pay these high taxes?" his father said to them. "Just so you can fart in your own yard and no one will hear? What's the point?"

"It's not so bad."

"Son, you keep feeding yourself those baloney sandwiches. That's okay. Right now, you think it's all pastrami on rye. Soon enough you're gonna realize, and you'll remember that you hate baloney."

His father had a point, but Jesse had Stacy, and that trumped everything.

Jesse zips up his jacket, pulls on his gloves and grabs his shovel. He steps into the snow that comes up above his ankles and sneaks in through the tops of his boots. He bends down and digs, lifts and throws. He repeats. And repeats. And repeats. He is already tired. His arms would rather be shoveling cereal into his mouth or resting on the sofa with the remote. He looks back to survey his progress. Barely a dent. He considers the length of the driveway and the time he has already spent. Why the hell didn't he move to the Keys?

Sonny is waving at Jesse from across the street. Jesse waves back. Sonny rests his shovel against his

Camaro and takes off his right glove. He digs into his jacket pocket for his Marlboros. He takes one out, pops it into his mouth and puts the pack back. He slips into his back pocket and pulls out a lighter. His hands must be numb, because the lighter jumps out when he tries to use it. He grabs it quickly and tries again. Sonny had once told Jesse that the only things he loved in life were his Camaro, his smokes and Dirty Harry movies. That was all there was to know about Sonny. That, and his kids never came to see him. Sometimes his wife, Anne Marie, would take off for a week here and there to go visit them, but they never came home. Jesse wasn't sure, but his best guess was that Sonny was close to sixty. Everything about him was thinning, gray and wrinkled. Even his elbows sagged.

Sonny smokes with his right hand and uses his left to wipe the snow off the trunk of his car. It doesn't fall far. Between what's fallen and what's been pushed up against it, the car is surrounded more than it's covered. Sonny blows smoke through his nose.

Jesse digs again. The sound of the shovel echoes through the snow-padded street. He hears another dig echoing back. It's Bruce, two doors down. He is wearing a blue knit Giants hat. Bruce is the only one who pays for lawn care instead of doing his own. Claims he's allergic to grass. They always cut it on an angle so it looks like it's going the wrong way. It's a nice, thick Buffalo grass with a fancy manicure suffocating to death under a heavy blanket of snow. Bruce also has a six-foot inflatable Santa on his roof and no chimney. Bruce digs. Jesse tosses. Sonny coughs. This goes on for several minutes, until they hear the distant rumbling of the snow plow.

"Sonuvabitch!" Sonny shouts.

"Should've put that thing on the driveway like I told you!" Jesse yells over to him.

"Sonuvagoddambitch."

Sonny stands in the road with his shovel. He looks like a soldier about to do battle. He stares dead-on at the plow coming at him, its giant blade like a big, open mouth saying, "Outta my way." It knocks a long wave of snow to its right, Sonny's side of the road. Sonny retreats and darts up the driveway. He watches the wave splash over the Camaro and drop in heavy clumps across his red hood. The plow leaves a pulverized track of dirty snow in its wake. Both of Sonny's right tires are buried again. He attacks the snow like a madman.

As Jesse digs, he can see Stacy's slender figure at their front door with a steaming mug of something in her hands. She leans against the frame, her pink, fuzzy foot holding the door ajar. Her face now is always the same. He looks away, back to the boundless white snows of subtopia. "Ready for a break yet?" he hears her say. But he's just getting warmed up out here. If he stops now, he won't want to start again. He'll curse himself tomorrow when he has to deal with two days worth of this shit.

They hadn't planned on moving into the suburbs, but it was the only district at the time that would hire such an inexperienced teacher, and she'd been born to teach. She'd always said that. She even has a teacher's name: Miss. Stacy. She was never Ms. Green, and she's definitely not a Mrs. Moran. Green is the color of snot, and Moran sounds too much like moron. Kids pick up on these sorts of things. Those inner-city kids would have destroyed her. She was an Upper East Side girl with an Upper West Side mentality. It was Stacy who'd really wanted this house. As soon as the idea came up, she'd leaped at it like it was a butterfly getting away. His office is in Garden City, so it's a commute for him either way.

Jesse shakes his head and gets back to work.

Bruce's kids come out and start messing up his lawn. They cut lines in the snow and ruffle it. His daughter makes a snow angel. Her legs and arms move up and down together like a puppet doing a dance. The boys, twins with curly hair and thick bodies, make forts out of the piles on either corner of the driveway Bruce has just finished clearing. One of them throws a snowball at the roof and hits Santa on the head. The other one shouts, "Score!"

It starts to snow again. Tiny drops of white polkadot Bruce's black-tarred driveway. Jesse has made it to the bottom of his, the dull gray cement showing cracks he's never noticed before. In his last dig, he pulls up something brown and clumpy. Must have been Mrs. Perlemutter's poodle, or whatever that thing is. He throws it into the street for the snow plow to find. It will only toss it back, but he sort of owns it now anyway. His property; his shit. He pays a lot of taxes for this.

He carves a path to the mailbox and uncovers it. It's empty. He hoists up the red flag. Stacy would give him hell for that, for wasting a man's time. But what does he care? The mailman always has to stop anyway. They get a dozen different catalogs a day, now that Christmas is coming.

Bruce is throwing down salt and yelling at his boys to stop throwing snowballs on the driveway. His blue hat is spotted with snow. Jesse holds out his gloved palm and collects a few flakes. It's picked up a bit, a heavier snowfall. He wonders how long he would have to stand there before he had a ball of his own, enough to throw. He and Stacy liked the idea of having kids. They would talk about it during Saturday morning cartoons. "One of these days," they would say. It would be good to have them on a day like today, to throw snowballs at them and teach them how to build snow forts. He wouldn't know what to do with them any other day.

Jesse's fingers are numb. He grabs his shovel and heads for the door to get that steaming mug of something into his hands. Then he hears the plow again. Sonny has given up on the car and has cleared a narrow path up the driveway. He's not going anywhere anyway.

Stacy greets him at the door. "Power's out," she tells him.

He takes off his wet, frozen gear and checks the thermostat. It's 68 now. He'll have to get the space heater out of the basement before it gets dark.

"Why don't we put up a tree?" Stacy says as he opens the basement door.

"Because we're not supposed to be here for Christmas," he responds.

Christmas. They were supposed to fly out to the West Coast to see his sister this year, their second Christmas together since they got married. Jesse's sister lives with some rich, old guy she met in Reno. City kid does good in the desert. She seems to have really thawed out over there. But this storm has frozen him. "Besides," he says, "I'm an atheist. I don't mind the gift-giving and the ho-ho-ho, but you know I don't go in for all that commercialized crap."

"We can toast marshmallows and roast chestnuts on the BBQ while we do it." Her enthusiasm is growing, and Jesse is concerned. This is sounding like too much trouble. He was going to take a bath and a nap and a shot of whiskey. "Come on," she pleads. "It'll be fun," she promises.

"We don't have a tree. Or chestnuts."

"We don't have chestnuts, but we have a yard full of trees." She gives him a Cheshire cat grin. "Don't we have an ax?" This is naughtiness coming from a third-grade teacher. Her face is always the same, but this is new. He kind of likes it.

Jesse goes down to the basement for the space heater and grabs his hacksaw off the wall. He wonders what the neighbors will say about him cutting down one of his trees. Maybe they won't notice. But they've got nothing else to do, and Mrs. Perlemutter next door is the kind to look out windows and ask questions. If he takes one from the other side of the house, only Sonny and Anne Marie might see, but they don't look out their windows. He doesn't know what they do.

Jesse leaves the heater and saw at the top of the stairs and goes back down to look for the box marked "Xmas". Before they were married, Stacy had another life with Christmas trees and expensive figurines of children playing jump rope and giving puppies bubble baths. It's all boxed up in their basement now, labeled carefully in case she wants to find it again.

She told him a story once about her first Christmas in her first apartment. She paid her own rent, and she was proud of that. Most of her friends were doing the trust fund baby shuffle in swanky Manhattan lofts, but she had a tiny studio near Brooklyn Heights with a basin by the bed, a toilet in a closet and a claw foot tub in the corner, no shower spray. She borrowed a little red wagon from some friends and pulled it five blocks to get a tree. She picked the most pathetic one, just so it wouldn't feel unloved. That's the sort of thing Stacy would do. She wheeled the thing back to her building without an elevator and left the wagon sitting on the stoop while she carried the tree up three flights of stairs. When she came back down to get the wagon, it was gone. "Why would someone want to steal a wagon?" she had asked him. He didn't know the answer. It wasn't something he would do. Stacy gave her friends ten bucks for the lost wagon, although they said they didn't mind that it was gone. They had a son, but he was in middle school by then, too big to be pulled. A few weeks later, Stacy saw a homeless man walking down Atlantic Avenue pulling a little red wagon full of junk.

He leaves Stacy in the living room with the Xmas box and puts his wet gear on again. The insides of his boots are ice cold. He and the hacksaw venture outside in search of a tree. At the back of their yard is the entrance to an unknown region he and Stacy always said they would explore, a small space of uncharted territory amid the subdivided urban sprawl. It is thick with dead trees and the occasional evergreen iced with heaping mounds of sugary snow. They own a very tiny bit of it, including a fruitless crab apple tree. It's a good size, but it's barren. Even in the spring, it only produces sour, worm-infested apples. Jesse isn't much for growing things. It was Sonny who'd told him what kind of tree it was. He'd also pointed out a small spruce by the side fence that had been a sapling from his own backyard, a gift to the people who once lived in Jesse's house after they had lost a much older one in a nor'easter. It would be nice to let that thing grow, Jesse thinks, to see how it changes, a little twig of proof that life finds a way. He keeps looking until he comes across a medium-sized juniper or cedar or anything green and sturdy enough to hang lights on, and he makes his first cut. The branches shake off their snow and say hello.

The blade on the saw is dull, and it gets stuck when he tries to pull it. His father had given him the saw when they'd bought this house. It was the same saw they'd used to make Jesse's go-carts when he was a kid. "Maybe you can build me a log cabin out on your prairie for when I get old," his dad had said. "I don't need some rusty saw mocking me with its teeth." Jesse jiggles it out now and cuts again until he has a deep enough cut to start slicing through. He goes at it, back and forth. The noise of the saw echoes through the yard. He stops and waits for the dead silence. Then he does it again, but this time, he can hear Bruce's voice coming from the front and over the fence.

"I said pack and roll, not roll and pack!" The boys

must be making snowmen. Jesse listens to the noises Mason and Jason make as they pack and roll. They are laughing and shouting. They are probably still rolling and packing. Jesse knows Bruce enough to know that he is annoyed because he likes things to be done efficiently. He used to be an area supervisor for one of the leading northeastern grocery stores. Stacy said his stores were the cleanest and most organized, but their produce wasn't always the freshest. And it wasn't the cheapest. She'd been to all of them, every Pathmark, every Waldbaums, every A&P in the area, but she'd drive a few extra miles out of her way to get the best produce. Jesse had to teach her how to drive when they moved out of the city. She loved it. She loved getting lost and finding her own way home. She bought her own car. A used Volvo. She even learned how to change her own tire, though she won't ever have to. Stacy's dad had given them an Automobile Club of America membership for her birthday last year.

Before he pulls at the saw again, he notices some movement in the trees. It's a doe digging around in the snow for some berries, or whatever they eat. Then another one, a baby, prances up beside it and digs its nose into the snow. Jesse makes a tiny "huh" sound. The doe fixes him with her eyes. She is watching him carefully, protecting her calf from the dangers he represents. Jesse hopes Stacy is seeing this. She loves it when the deer saunter into the yard. She never had these moments in her former life. Snow White in the big city. Jesse and the doe make eyes at each other, and in that moment, there is nothing else. The calf is unaware of his presence, its little head busy poking and prodding for goodies hidden in the snow. Jesse wants to turn around and see Stacy watching this through the window, but he stays frozen, eyes fixed on the life in front of him.

The sound of a horn echoes through the trees, startling the deer, and they run off, back into the woods they came from. Jesse leaves the saw sticking out of the side of the tree and goes over to the fence. He sees Sonny standing in the middle of the street smoking a cigarette. His left arm is resting on the top of his shovel, and his Camaro is now completely cleared of snow. The snow plow is idling two feet in front of him.

"Pull up your plow," Sonny shouts. "Or plow me down."

The plow driver rolls down his window. "This is county business you're obstructing," he says.

"I'm a taxpayer. I pay your salary. And I'm telling you to pull up your plow."

Jesse looks over and sees that Bruce is also watching this suburban showdown.

"You pull up the plow, you can pass," Sonny says. "Otherwise, we'll both stand here till we freeze to death."

That was a bad move, thinks Jesse. The plow driver is in a heated cab. Jesse can see him talking on a radio, probably notifying dispatch to call the police. He could be arrested for this. He'll never win. He knows it, too. What the hell's wrong with him?

Jesse undoes the latch on the gate and shoves it open just enough to squeeze through. He makes big holes in the snow with his feet, snow scrunching loudly as he moves, and gets himself into the street.

Bruce sees Jesse coming and tells his kids to go inside and get some hot cocoa from their mother. He walks over to the plow and knocks on the window to talk to the plowman, nodding at Jesse, a signal to handle the old man.

Sonny lights up another cigarette.

"What's up?" Jesse says.

"This sonuvabitch won't go around," Sonny tells him.

"It's his job, Sonny."

"I know it's his job, but all I want is for him to not plow in this tiny bit of space. Is that so much?"

Bruce walks over to Sonny and Jesse. "The guy says he'll pull up the plow," he tells them, "if you'll agree to move your car out of the street before he comes back."

"What do you say, Sonny?" asks Jesse. It's a fair proposal. But Sonny doesn't think so.

"I don't give a damn what he says. I'm not moving that car."

Jesse doesn't know why this is such an issue, but Sonny is funny about that car, and he hates being told what to do. When Jesse saw him yesterday and mentioned the forecast, Sonny shrugged and said he didn't do things according to plans, God's or anybody's.

"Why don't you just move the car?" Bruce asks.

"Where am I going to put it?"

"You can park it on my driveway until yours is cleared," Jesse tells him. Sonny doesn't respond. He just stares at the plow without really looking at it. The plowman honks his horn again. Jesse offers to help shovel Sonny's driveway, but Sonny says he can do it himself, he's just not in the mood. Jesse isn't sure what he wants from all this. This is one of those things Stacy could figure out. She would play Connect the Dots with things Jesse didn't even notice and come up with a picture of something he could recognize, a kitten or a tea kettle, but was unable to see on his own. All he could see was a stubborn old man.

"Let's not be ridiculous, Sonny," Bruce says.

At this, Sonny lets go of his shovel and punches Bruce in the face. Jesse grabs Sonny's arms to hold him back, but he's limp, arms like sticks, and Jesse can feel his muscles twitching around his bones in fear. Bruce has his hand over his nose and he's growling like a pissed-off dog. He gives Sonny a look that reminds him of how frail he is, how hard it is to knock a man like Bruce to the ground, and how easy it would be for Bruce to return that punch.

"Christ," Sonny says.

Jesse can feel Sonny's arms relax. He lets him go.

"Sorry, Brucey boy," Sonny says with his hand out. "I didn't mean to do that."

Bruce takes his hand away from his face, but he doesn't take up Sonny's handshake. His nose is bleeding. His palm is smeared with blood. A cloud of white steam blows from out of his mouth.

Jesse notices for the first time today that he is awake. He's seen blood before. He's seen a man punch another man, sometimes without provocation, many times more than once. But this shocks him. Blood drips from Bruce's nose and Jesse watches it hit the snow. It dissolves from crimson to cherry red to bright pink. Something about the color of it coming from a human body amazes him. Why is it so beautiful, he wonders. It's such a terrible lie. He starts to feel sick. The plowman honks his horn again.

"I'll move the car," Sonny says in a way that makes it clear he hasn't resigned, he's just taken a while to make up his mind.

Jesse thinks about the last time he spoke to his father. He'd asked Jesse why he was still living all the way the hell out there with the ponies.

"Do you mean phonies, Dad?"

"No, son, I mean ponies. People who let assholes take them for a ride."

Sonny tosses his lit cigarette into the snow. It sizzles as it goes out.

"He needs some help," Bruce says to Jesse.

"I'll help him," Jesse says.

"That ain't what I mean."

"He is what he is," Jesse says. "It hard for him."

"It's hard for everyone."

"How bad is it?"

"I'll live." Bruce pulls his cap off and rubs the blood from his nose with it. "He should name that piece of junk Loretta," he says pointing to Sonny's Camaro. He turns to the plowman and nods his head before walking back to his house and disappearing inside.

The plow lifts off the ground. "I don't know what came over me," Sonny says to Jesse as they move off the road to let the plowman pass. The plow's engine revs and the truck slowly drives past Sonny's car. It stops, drops its plow, and continues down the road. "I couldn't have broken it, an old man like me. But what a sting."

Sonny gets into his Camaro and starts it up. Jesse pushes it free from the rear, and it pulls up over the snow before the engine dies. It's too cold. Sonny starts it up again.

Jesse knocks on the passenger window. "Let it run," Jesse shouts. "He probably won't be back down again for another ten or twenty." Sonny reaches over and unlocks the door. Jesse gets in. It smells like vanilla and leather protector. The seat is cold and hard.

"I'm sorry about that," Sonny says. He switches the heat on and opens the vents. Cold air blows on Jesse's arms and legs. "Bruce can be an ass sometimes, but he didn't deserve that."

Jesse puts his hand on the door handle. "Forget about it," he says, his fingers tense and ready to pull. "Don't let it spoil your Christmas."

"He's not like us," Sonny continues. "He doesn't understand."

Jesse turns his head and glances out the window. Sonny's house doesn't look real. It looks more like a cheap oil painting in a market, something hung on a wall in a nursing home. There are no lights on, no signs of life. Just an ordinary two-story brick house covered in snow. And then Jesse notices it, the dot he had failed to connect: Sonny's empty driveway with the trail he had made from his door to his car.

"Where's Anne Marie?" he asks.

"Gone," Sonny says. He puffs on his cigarette.

"Been gone since Thanksgiving. She says she won't come home for another lonely Christmas without her family."

Jesse isn't sure how to respond. "I'm sorry," is all he can think to say. He doesn't know anything about Sonny's problems. Anne Marie and Stacy used to talk sometimes, but Stacy never bothered to share. She knew he didn't want to get involved. That's not how city boys are.

"I'm the sorry one," Sonny says to him. "But you know how it is. I feel for you, Jess. Ain't much fun rattling around in a big house all alone." He lights another cigarette. "It's fucking Christmas." A cloud of gray smoke follows his words.

Jesse had told his dad that he liked being a pony because it gave him some reason to keep going. "That race is over, kid," said his father. "And you didn't win." Jesse digs for something to say to Sonny, but his bag isn't big enough. He has no tricks for the old man. If this was a prairie, they would probably both be shot.

"When I was your age," Sonny says, "I thought there'd be more than this." Jesse thinks he smells liquor, but maybe it's the Armor All on the seats. "This is it for me." He puts the car in gear. "Maybe you've still got a chance," he says before giving the car some gas and rolling it over the snow. He's careful not to let it slide as he turns into Jesse's driveway and parks it where the Volvo used to sit. "All I've got is this car," he says, "and she ain't going nowhere." He grabs Jesse's arm. "I'm glad you stuck around, kid," he says.

"Actually, I'm thinking it might be time to move

on."

"You don't need to," Sonny says, his hold on Jesse getting tighter. "Just take your time."

"With what?" Jesse asks.

"With whatever it is," Sonny says. He lets go of Jesse and looks out the window at the house in front of them. "She might not be ready to go yet either."

Jesse bangs the snow off his boots and leaves them outside on the porch. The power's back, but it's still cold in the house. *The Bells of Saint Mary's* is on the TV. Stacy would be watching this, he thinks. She'd be curled up on the couch in her pink, fuzzy slippers with a steaming mug of something in her warm hands. She had told him once that Bing Crosby reminded her of her grandfather. Jesse has seen pictures of him, but he'd never heard his voice. He died long before Jesse met Stacy, so Jesse didn't know what it was that Stacy thought of when she thought of him, other than Bing Crosby. Her grandfather was from her former life, the one Jesse had only heard about from the memories Stacy would share, the stories that had started to come back to him, filling up the vacant spaces of their home and keeping him going. In every room, there were traces of moments and so many gaps he couldn't fill. Empty pages of the plot. But he knew how the story ended: with a house in the suburbs and a Volvo that crushes like a tin can. And blood. Blood that once filled her body and kept her warm. Blood that had been left to seep deep into the road. Blood that has gone cold.

The thought of Bruce's blood in the road makes

Jesse queasy again. Maybe he will move on, he thinks. Maybe tomorrow or the next day or one day next year, but not today. Today, he still needs to be right here.

He opens the Xmas box and digs through Stacy's past. It's full of colorful balls and little wooden drummer boys on strings. He pulls out an angel with red hair and fluffy wings. This is just like Stacy, he thinks. Red hair and all.

He goes into the kitchen and something out the back window catches his eye. He sees the tail of the doe waving goodbye as she runs away again. She is gone. Jesse knows she is never coming back. It's time for her to move on.

He sees the tree with the saw in its side, and it makes him sad. Stacy would have hated that. He got that one wrong.

He goes outside and gently pulls out the hacksaw and places the angel on top of the tree. That's better, he thinks. She would have liked that. A little tree in her own yard, no more missing wagons, and a redheaded angel watching over him.

WORLD ON A STRING

Memories are all I have to cling to,
And heartaches are the friends I'm talking to.
~ Dean Martin
"Things"

Hank had himself a good little lawn, not too big, not too small. Sixteen square feet of Kentucky Bluegrass green, four by four by four by four. Just right. Anything more would have been too much trouble for a man of Hank's temperament and grace. Or so his son had said. Hank didn't necessarily see it that way, but he wasn't in the business of calculating grace. Just lawns. Hank had his ways. That was true. His son thought it was a talent to drive a cab for so many years and never figure out how to give or take direction. There was a fault, his son had told him more than a few times, in the way Hank listened. But Hank had heard plenty of things. Some of them made no sense to him. That was the problem. Hank hated people who talked about shit he knew nothing about as if he knew what they were saying. Hank also hated crying and certain kinds of laughter, gum chewing, spitting, dogs in sweaters, Oprah Winfrey, cold butter on toast and rap music. He didn't need reasons. He just did.

His son called him an ornery, intolerant, monotonous bastard. He said he needed to get out more, meet new people, experience new things. Hank said he was too old for new things. He already had everything he needed: a son out in the burbs, a daughter out in Vegas, one ex-wife almost far enough away and another in an urn on top of the TV. He wasn't alone; he just didn't have someone around to iron his clothes and ask him for money.

Hank knew what day it was by simple rotation: Sunday was mass; Monday was Pathmark; Tuesday was bingo; Wednesday was the laundromat; Thursday was lawn bowling at the Lions Club; Friday was *Law & Order*; and Saturday was spaghetti. If he was out of clean socks, it was hump day. If he found himself down on his knees, it was Sunday. But every day was his good little lawn, which always needed raking, or watering, or mowing with the weed whacker or a simple, "Hello, you sweet sack of sod." Hank also had an old oak tree standing between his street and the sidewalk that shat too many damn acorns and leaves and a neighbor, Mrs. Manischewitz, who thought he was the spawn of Satan. But Hank knew she was wrong, because Satan would never live in a Jewish neighborhood. Every day, too, was Mrs. Manischewitz sitting on her stoop in her housecoat waiting for Death to come and get her. "He's just over on Avenue U picking up the lox and bagels, Mrs. Manischewitz," Hank would say to her with a wave. She was deaf like a spider. Eight eyes everywhere but on him. But he knew she knew he was there. One particularly hazy, hot and humid day, Hank had decided to water his grass in his swimming trunks, and she went inside and watched the street from the window instead, coughing up something into that befouled snot rag she always had in her hand. Every day, Hank would be out on his lawn, smiling and waving. And every day, Mrs. Manischewitz would look away. She never once gave him a smile, or a nod or a wink. Not even a glance. It was always the same, every day. "Still chipper as a pallbearer," Hank would say. "And still not dead."

But then one day, all that changed. Hank's lawn was still there, but Mrs. Manischewitz was dead. It was a Tuesday. Bingo!

Two weeks later, the son and daughter-in-law came to clear out the house, and the daughter-in-law, who was a converted gentile, a goy in Jew's clothing, told Hank about the stroke, the pneumonia and the phone call in the middle of the night. She also told him about the fights. This was none of Hank's business, but she'd caught him there, out on his lawn, and he had to wait until she was done with her own little episode of *60 Minutes* before he could get away. There was a home up in Westchester, she'd told him, a nice place, lots of Jews and Scrabble. It was close to where they lived. They could visit on weekends. But she'd refused. She wasn't going to leave her home for anyone but Death. She'd probably still be alive, the daughter-in-law said, had she only. They'd begged and pleaded, the daughter-in-law told him. Then she sighed. "Such mishugina," she said, "you don't know."

The daughter-in-law seemed to hate the stingy shviger more than he did. Nobody knew how much she had or where she kept it. There was a will, but not much was in it. Even dead, she didn't want people to know her business. And then there was all the schlock and photographs no one knew had existed hidden under chests of drawers and sofa cushions. There was an attic filled with useless crap and too many bitter memories, clippings from old newspapers from as far back as the Johnson administration. There was even a can of sauerkraut that had expired sometime during the Cold War. It was like a mausoleum for insignificant things in there, the daughter-in-law had said. Lifeless, unwanted, rotting things.

On the last day of the clearing out, the son knocked on Hank's door and asked if he'd be interested in her shrubbery. The son's name was Barry. He was a dentist. He had nice teeth and a nose like a shark. "She's got a potted hyacinth," he said to Hank. "You could put it down out here. Would look nice."

"I don't really have what you'd call a floral garden, Dr. Manischewitz," Hank said.

"Moskowitz," said Barry.

"I could maybe give it to my son," Hank said. "He's got more real estate than me. Lives out in the burbs. On Long Island."

"What about house plants? There's a few African violets, a Boston fern and an eternity plant." The tip of his nose bobbed up and down when he spoke.

"I don't need anything that's going to outlast me," Hank said. He felt his stomach rumble. He could smell mothballs. He thought about going to Finkel's for bratwurst before bingo. He could see the empty stoop in the distance. "Why don't you just leave whatever you've got right here," he said to Dr. Sharknose. "I'll do something with it."

He told his son everything he knew, that they were selling or renting, not moving in, because they had no use for Brooklyn anymore, now the old gargoyle was gone. "Did you know they were Moskowitz?" Hank said.

"Everyone knew they were Moskowitz," said his son.

"Well nobody told me. Anyhow, he's got a big place up in Westchester now, the son, you know. He's like you."

"In no way at all is Barry Moskowitz anything like me, Dad."

"Yeah, well, they're doing some renovations on the place first. I don't know what. That's none of my business. 'They shouldn't disturb you too much,' says Finface. We'll see about that."

The renovators came on a Tuesday and left on a Thursday. The real estate agent with the young couples and their baby carriages came every day until the For Sale sign was gone. That was when the Virgin Mary appeared on the stoop and Hank almost wet himself. It was a Monday. Something had happened while he was down at the Pathmark buying his veal cutlets.

"Twenty-seven years I've been the only Mick on this block," he said to his son. "I don't know which is worse — that old vision of hell Manimoskowitz or the constant reminder that I'm going there."

His son told him to go say hello, invite them over

for coffee. It'd give him a reason to clean up the house a little.

"There's nothing wrong with my house," Hank said.

"Okay. But you could at least be friendly. They're your neighbors."

"All I'm saying is this is my turf. I get all the leftover latkes around here."

"They could be very nice people."

"Very nice people, my ass. They're Catholics, son. We're not a friendly lot."

Hank had twisted himself up in the phone cord pacing around the kitchen trying to look out the kitchen window (which was, he had to admit, indecent). He'd heard some noises coming from Mrs. Manimoskowitz's backyard. He couldn't see anything over the high fence that had served as a division for many years between his backyard and the sight of the old bat's nether regions when she was bent over her geraniums, but he'd heard the definite sounds of something. Something was going on over there. "I'm hanging up now, son."

Hank unwound himself and went upstairs to the back bedroom. He tripped over a dumbbell, stubbed his big toe on the edge of the bed and took the Lord's name in vain several times before he made it to the window. And there she was: the new Mrs. Manimoskowitz. She wasn't very old, but she wasn't very young, either. She was pale and thin with bright red lips and black buttons for eyes. It wouldn't have bothered him so much if she'd been tending to the geraniums. He watched her hang two pillowcases, some nylons and a nightgown on the line

131

with some clothespins she had clipped to her apron. It wasn't any of his business what she hung on her line, but Hank knew which way the sun shined. The dingbat had hung her line the wrong way.

Then Hank's eyes wandered into his own backyard, with its weeds seeping through the cracks in the cement, his decrepit picnic table, his old fishing pole, a pair of shoes he'd meant to clean after stepping in some fresh dog shit and several houseplants, now just as dead as their previous owner. He'd taken them back there and forgotten all about them. "Christ Almighty," he said. "I've been looking for that pole."

The following Monday, on his way home from Pathmark, Hank stopped at Abraham's for a little smoked salmon to go with his baked potato, and he bumped into Mrs. Gershon from up the street, who hadn't heard anything yet about the new Mrs. Manimoskowitz (Who knew bupkis of their neighbors these days?), but who had some kugel left over from Shabbat, if he was interested.

After Hank had finished eating his kugel, he went into the backyard to clean the dog shit off his shoes. He heard talking. Red Lips had company. "I can see you there," she was saying. "Yes, I do. Hello there."

Hank peeked through the cracks in the fence.

"Aren't you handsome?" Red Lips said.

Hank didn't know who she was talking to. Far as he could tell, there was no one else there. "Just my fucking luck," he said to himself. "Another one of *those*."

The next day, a Tuesday, Hank woke up with a

start. He checked his pulse, felt his groin and let out a
fart. It wasn't his heart or the kugel. It wasn't Death
standing over him. But it was something. Something had
stirred him.

"Birds, son!" Hank shouted over the phone. "Birds!
Birds, birds!"

The new Mrs. Manimoskowitz had put up a bird
feeder in her backyard that had summoned birds from
every continent to come squawking at Hank's window
before the sun came up. Fresh droppings had collected
on his window ledge. The refuse of a nest was clogging
up his drainpipes. Hank had moved into the front
bedroom, then down to the sofa, but they were
everywhere, the fucking birds, with their damn
squawking.

"Oh, come on," said his son.

"Don't you 'oh, come on' me," Hank said. "Do you
know what this means?"

It meant war. It meant many battles and a whole lot
of sharp words that Hank would unleash on his innocent
(and very patient) son at six in the morning. It meant
purple bird shit all over everything and blackberries
spreading out of the Levinson yard like a florid, seedy
disease.

Hank saw her through the front window hanging
balls of birdseed in that old oak tree that already shat too
many acorns and leaves. It was none of Hank's business
what she did in her own yard, but that wasn't even her
tree.

"It's not yours either, Dad."

"She's breaking the law."

"I doubt that."

"I'm cutting it down. Right on top of her."

"*That* would be breaking the law."

"She's stealing all your birds, son. Birds belong with you, out in the burbs."

"We've still got plenty. Don't worry about us."

"I'm not worried. I'm just saying. They're tearing up my grass, for Christ's sake."

"I don't know what you want me to say, Dad."

"Does rat poison work on birds?"

"I don't know."

"Maybe I can shoot them."

Hank didn't have a gun or a license to get one. Sid, his bingo buddy, had told him that things killed by poison were usually more of a problem after they were dead, the stench of their rotting flesh hidden in the hollows of walls and floorboards haunting their killers for months, sometimes years. "So, you'll get used to the birds," Sid had said. "Take it from me. My wife talks in her sleep. 'You forgot to lock the gate again, Sidney. Not in front of Mrs. Levine, Sidney.' Forty-eight years of this, day and night. You learn to ignore." But Hank didn't want ignorance. He wanted peace. He wanted silence. He wanted sleep. He couldn't imagine forty-eight years of this. He had barely lived through three days of it. He rang the local precinct. There was very little they could do about the birds.

"What about singing?"

"Singing?"

"She sings."

"What kind of singing are we talking about?"

"What kind is there? Singing. You know. *I've got the world on a string. I'm sitting on a rainbow.* Shit like that. In the backyard."

"Is it very loud?"

"I can hear it."

"But it would have to be extremely loud, Mr. Moran."

"How loud?"

"Operatic."

"She's no Pavarotti, I'll tell you that much."

The law was not on his side, but it was sympathetic. They suggested he purchase a pair of ear plugs. They didn't have any advice about his lawn.

On Wednesday, Hank came home from the laundromat and found a little fat boy sitting on the stoop with the virgin. He had a bouncy ball, one of those rubber jobs the kids get from the vending machines at Pathmark. Thinking about Pathmark, Hank realized he'd left his new box of fabric softener sheets, the only ones he likes to use for his towels, at the Coin Wash. When Hank came back from retrieving his fabric softener, the boy was gone, but there was old Red Lips, waving at him from the stoop. She shouted over to him and introduced herself, said her name was Nettle or something, and apologized for not coming over, but all the unpacking and settling in, it's not so easy for a woman her age, he could imagine, and with her grandson coming to visit soon and she couldn't find the box with the pillowcases but they were already in the linen closet the whole time, could he believe that?

Hank nodded. He couldn't keep up. She was like

the inside of a vacuum cleaner with all sorts of fuzz flying around. There was something about a broken window and something else about a train. Hank didn't know what it was. He just nodded. Got inside as quick as he could. Away from the chatty dingbat.

He saw her again the next day, Thursday, on his way home from the Lions Club. He could see her and her red lips as soon as he turned the corner. She was standing in front of that damn tree. In front of his damn house! There was no way to avoid her. Unless he went over to the next block and asked the Goldbergs if he could borrow a ladder to climb over the fence. But Hank didn't have time for that. His bladder was too occupied for gymnastics.

She didn't notice him at first. She had her attention up in the branches. It looked like she was talking to the tree, probably telling it how to fall over and crush him as he passed. As he got closer, Hank could hear that she was whistling. Very softly. She was whistling into that damn tree. He tried to slip past her. But it was too late. She'd seen him. "Hello again, neighbor," she said. "I'm singing to the eggs." She pointed up into the tree. "There's a new nest. I think it's the robins."

Hank didn't care. He wasn't happy about her being out there in front of his lawn. He wasn't looking forward to dealing with a bunch of chirping baby birds, but he didn't have time for it now. Nor did he have time to hear about her pillowcases. It was none of his business where she hung her sheets. "Can't chat now," he said. "My prostate." He made his escape.

And then, on Friday, the banging began.

"It's coming from the kitchen," Hank told his son. "She must be hacking something to bits in there. Children maybe."

"Dad, she isn't doing anything wrong. You're being hypersensitive."

"I'm not being any kind of sensitive."

"You'll adjust."

"Not before she kills me."

With that, Hank's doorbell rang.

"Hang on, son."

From the front window, he could see Red Lips there on the stoop.

"Yoohoo!" She waved at him.

"Mercy me. She's here."

"Be nice."

"If I don't pick up the phone tomorrow, call the police."

"Hello there!" she said when Hank opened the door. She had a little blue hat on and a box of Entenmann's. "It's Moron, isn't it?"

"What?"

"It says Moron on your mailbox here."

"That's Moran," Hank said, his thick pointer finger tapping away. "That's an 'a' there."

"Is it?"

There was no question. It was. "Name's Hank MORAN."

"I see." She held out her hand. "Nicoletta Dupree. We met the other day. My friends call me Netta."

"Dupree... that's French, ain't it? We don't have any French frogs on this street."

Red Lips laughed. Hank didn't. He had a flounder waiting for him on the counter in the kitchen.

"Dupree is my married name," she said, like he *was* a moron. "I used to be a Pizzarelli."

"A dago, eh? We had some dagos here a few years back. A young couple. From Gravesend, I think."

Netta perked up. "I'm from Gravesend," she said. "Grew up right on Ocean Parkway."

"You don't say?"

"Yes," she said. "But that was many, many years ago." And then she said something about a drug store and an ice cream shop and a kiss on the subway and the Wonder Wheel at Coney Island and had he ever been on it?

"Who hasn't?" Hank said.

And then there was something about a broken window and the Poconos. Hank couldn't keep up. Again with the Electrolux and all the fluff flying around, or maybe it was the gnats and mosquitoes or those damn birds, he didn't know. Squawk, squawk, squawk. It was because of her gynecologist, she was saying. It was all because she had been to the gynecologist, and when she was in the examination room, on the table, suddenly she smelled Nathan's hot dogs, and this made her think about Coney Island and the Wonder Wheel and her father, who did something with birds, and having her first ride on the Wonder Wheel and the smell of the hot dogs made her think how much she missed it and eating hot dogs and birds but not eating the birds and so she decided to come home. Then she started with the damn signing again. *If you've been a rover, journey's end lies over the Brooklyn Bridge.* It was Sinatra, she was saying, it was Sinatra who'd been singing and she'd heard it while she was on the table at the gynecologist's office, legs akimbo, and it had made her think about the hot dogs. That's what it was, she told him. Frank Sinatra and hot dogs, she said. Even though it was none of his damn business.

"You done?" Hank said, though not out loud.

"I have a leak," she said.

"A leak?"

"In the kitchen. Under the sink."

"That's too bad."

"I was wondering if perhaps you could come have a peek."

"Why would I want to do that?"

"Oh!" she said. She thought he was being funny.

This was just what he needed. A leaky damsel in distress at the door on *Law & Order* night. He didn't have time for this. He had a flounder on the counter waiting for him.

"I'm not a plumber," Hank said.

"I thought, being a man, most men are usually handy, aren't they? It will only take a minute. Maybe something needs screwing."

"What about your husband?" Hank said, only then thinking he hadn't noticed a Mr. Red Lips.

"I'm afraid he's gone," she said.

Gone? Gone where? Gone to Arby's? Gone to Texas?

"It's just me in the house," she said. "And I'm hopeless with these sorts of things."

139

"I'm sorry," Hank said. He didn't know why. It didn't mean anything. He couldn't imagine it was anything too serious, what with all that renovating they'd just done over there. But what did he know? He'd driven a cab for thirty-two years. Sinks weren't his thing. "Might just need a new washer or something," he said. Maybe that was enough to get her to go away.

"I take it you don't mean me," she said.

"That depends," said Hank. "How old are you?"

"Sixty," she said.

"Well, I can't speak for you or your sink, Mrs. Dupree, but I'd recommend you call a plumber. Now if you'll excuse me, I have a fish to fry. It's been nice meeting you."

"Netta," she said. "Please. My friends call me Netta."

Friends? When did that happen? Next she'll be wanting to come over and use his shower, eat his ice cream, soak her bra and panties in his tub, things that were none of his business.

"How many sinks you got?" he said.

"How many?"

"Some of these Jewish houses, they've got two. If you've got a second one, you can use that."

"This one only has the one," she said.

"That's too bad," Hank said. "They were Jews. The people who lived in there before you."

"Oh!" she said, again thinking he was being funny. Then she launched another one of her verbal tirades, asking him how well he knew Mrs. Manimoskowitz and telling him there was an old photograph she'd found in the house and she was very curious who the young woman in the photo was and then there was some long story about a painting of some lady whose husband had gone away somewhere and while he was gone his wife came down with a bad illness like the plague or scarlet fever or something and was in a coma for a long, long time and when she finally woke up she claimed she wasn't in a coma at all but living another life somewhere and in this other life she spoke Spanish and was married to another man she said she didn't know her real husband, had never set eyes on him before, and somehow, without having had any way or reason to learn Spanish before she was in the coma, the woman could speak it fluently and the husband couldn't convince her it was only a dream, so he had someone paint this portrait of her, because he knew that, eventually, she was going to leave him, but in the painting, all the husband could see was the longing in her eyes for the other husband, the Spanish one, and something about that photo reminded her of that painting. She showed Hank the photo. The woman looked familiar, but Hank told her he had no idea who she was. Hank said there probably wasn't anything much he could tell her about anything, sinks included.

Netta thanked him anyhow and then, finally, she went away and Hank ate his flounder and watched his *Law & Order* in peace.

Saturday came, and Hank decided to wash the windows, but he was out of Windex, so he went across the street to Nancy Nussbaum to borrow a bissel. Instead, she gave him a dirty look and just a bisseleh of some kosher knock-off stuff. "It wasn't even blue, this shit," Hank told his son. "'What about green?' I says to her. 'You got anything in that color spectrum? I'll take something green.' But no. She gives me this shit, smells like a pickled egg. You know anything about this?"

"Nope," said his son.

"Well, I'm not gonna use it."

"Why not?"

"Because of the birds."

Silence.

"Hello?" Hank said.

"What do you mean — because of the birds? That doesn't even make sense."

"Look, I spray this shit on my windows, my windows smell like this shit. These birds old Red Lips has flying around here smell it, think it's candy, and they come to my window with their squawking, all pissed off at me because instead of Windex, I get a bisseleh of this shit."

"What?"

"That's why Windex don't smell nothing like food. You see?"

Silence.

"What's wrong with you today anyway? You have a hot date keeping you up all night or something?"

"Kind of."

"Oh shit."

"Now what?"

"There's that fat kid again. He's climbing up my damn tree. I'll call you back later."

Hank rushed out to stop the fat kid from breaking

branches and sending acorns and shit all over his lawn, but the kid was gone by the time he got there. He'd left plenty of evidence, though. Acorns and leaves and shit everywhere.

As Hank was heading into the garage for his rake, a yellow cab pulled up, and Red Lips came out of her house and waved to the cabbie. Then she saw Hank and waved to him too. "Beautiful day to be working in the yard," she said with her big red grin.

Hank grumbled.

"I'm off to Coney Island to have a hot dog," she said. She was standing next to the cab now, door open, like she was waiting for something else to happen. "Would you like to join me?" she said.

Hank grumbled again. Then he realized what she'd meant. "That's very kind of you and all," he said, "but I've got a lot to do."

"What do you have to do that can't wait?" she said, as if it was her business. "Who doesn't have time for a Nathan's hot dog and the Wonder Wheel?"

"Oh," said Hank. "No, I don't do anything where I might lose my lunch. Defeats the purpose of eating it in the first place. No, you go on ahead. I'm fine here with my raking."

"Are you sure?" she said. "Not even for the hot dog?"

It was Saturday. Saturday was spaghetti. It wasn't go out to Coney Island with a dingbat for a nice case of agita day. "Go on," said Hank. "Enjoy.

Red Lips hopped into her cab and took off. Hank finished up his raking, thinking about her sitting on that stupid Ferris wheel all by herself.

And then he was there again. The little fat kid. He'd somehow managed to climb all the way out to the middle of a branch that was bowing from the weight of him. "Hey!" Hank shouted. "Hey, you! Get the hell outta there! You're too fat for that branch. Can't you see? You wanna kill yourself? You're shaking crap all over the place. I just raked here!"

The little fat kid didn't seem to notice Hank. He was stretched out across the limb, reaching for something on a branch above it. His shirt had rolled up past his fat little belly.

"Hey, kid!" Hank said. "You deaf or just dumb?"

The little fat kid looked at Hank for a second. Then he went back to his business, whatever it was.

"I'll call the police," Hank said.

But the kid didn't budge. He just lay there on that branch up in that damn tree. He reminded Hank of a boy he used to know, way back, a long, long time ago. Fatty Frankie, they called him. Hank couldn't remember his real name. He was a short, pudgy kid with tight curly hair and dark eyes, dumb as a stick and lousy at stickball. A real putz, if Hank ever knew one. Nobody ever wanted to play with Fatty Frankie. They would hide in their houses whenever they saw him coming and say there was nobody home when he rang the doorbell. And the kid would just walk away and say nothing. Not even, "I know you're in there." When they beat him up, he would cry a little, but he never said a thing. Not to no one. The last time Hank saw him was right after high school. He wasn't short and pudgy anymore by then, but he still had the same curls and dumb head. He'd told Hank he had tried to join the Army, but they wouldn't let him in. Said something about having flat feet. He was trying to get a job working for the city instead. Then a few years later, Hank heard Fatty Frankie had locked himself in his garage and shot himself in that dumb head of his with his father's hunting rifle. Hank didn't know if it was true, but it sounded about right to him.

Hank had never seen this fat kid before. Except for Wednesday, when he was on the porch with the virgin. "Hey, kid," he said. "Do you like fishing? I've got a pole in the back I can give ya, if you come down from there. I'll give it to you. Do you know how to fish?"

The little fat kid shook his head.

"If you come down outta that tree right now, I'll show you how to bait a worm. You like slimy things?"

The little fat kid nodded. Then he twisted himself around and began to make his way off the branch. Then there was a snap.

"Look out, Fatty!" Hank shouted.

The kid grabbed the branch above him just as his branch began to drop. He swung there like a monkey, his legs flailing about.

"I told you that was a dumb idea, didn't I, kid?" Hank said.

And just as the kid let go of the upper branch, both he and the thing he had been trying to reach fell out of the tree and landed right on Hank's feet. "Well I'll be a son of a bitch," Hank said. "Look at this mess." But the little fat kid was already gone. "Pretty fast for a fat boy."

Hank went into his garage and got his gardening

145

gloves. He put them on and shoved his hands into a bag of potting soil. He smeared the soil all over his gloves. Then he went back out to the tree and turned over the fallen nest. There were three eggs. Only one of them had broken. Hank carefully lifted the nest, gently prodding the uncracked eggs back in, and brought it over to the tree. He found a nice, safe branch, pulled it down, put the nest in it snug as he could, and gently brought the branch up again. He cleaned up the broken egg mess with Nancy Nussbaum's kosher window cleaner. Then he went back into his house, ate his spaghetti, and fell asleep on the couch, stinking like potting soil and pickled egg.

When he woke up on Sunday morning, Hank thought he heard chirping. But there was nothing. Just silence. Not a peep.

"She tried to kill me yesterday," he told his son.

"Oh really? How?"

"With the Wonder Wheel," Hank said.

"Seriously?"

"Yes, seriously. But I'm too smart for her. Gotta be careful with those Eyetalians, you know."

"So you've said."

Hank could see her out there through the window, whistling to the nest in the tree.

"Did I ever tell you about Fatty Frankie," Hank said.

"Who?"

Hank saw Red Lips go up on her tiptoes. She was trying to get a peek inside, see if the eggs were still there.

"This kid, Fatty Frankie," Hank said. "I haven't thought about him in years."

"What's brought him up now?"

Hank bent down and put his ear closer to the window. There were some body parts from a dead fly melted to the screen, some poor bastard who'd gotten trapped in there over the winter.

"Yo?" said Hank's son. "You die on me?"

"No, I'm here."

"You went quiet. You're distracted. What's going on over there?"

"Nothing, nothing. Just looking at something. Let me call you back."

Hank put the phone down. He opened the window and saw several of the dead fly's buddies in the sill, flat on their backs. Then he heard the chirping, little peeps, coming from outside. And singing. *What a lovely view from, Heaven looks at you from the Brooklyn Bridge...*

Hank closed the window. The potting soil had done the trick. He picked up the phone. "So I never told you about Fatty Frankie, eh?"

"No," said his son.

"Never told you the story of the time some punks from Red Hook came and chased him up into a tree and he stayed in there all night?"

"No. Never. You never tell me these stories."

"Well, there's one for ya," Hank said. He sat down on the sofa and looked out at his good little lawn and the tree that shat too many acorns and leaves. Something didn't seem right.

"What about the attempted murder on the Wonder

Wheel story?" said his son. "You ever gonna tell me that one?"

"That was it."

"That's it? That's all you're gonna tell me? She tried to kill you with the Wonder Wheel. The end."

"No, not 'the end'. Nobody says 'the end' at the end of a story."

"Then what do they say?"

"They say nothing. I stop talking, then that's it. End of story."

Red Lips had disappeared, probably back into her own birdhouse for some worms to feed the kids.

"Hello?" Hank's son said.

"Yeah, what?" said Hank.

"What is up with you today?"

"Nothing. I'm fine. I'm just busy. What's it to you?"

"Never mind. Back to business. I'll talk to you tomorrow."

Hank hung up the phone. He had nothing else to say. Fatty Frankie was dead. The end. He went out back and got his old fishing pole so he could get it ready for the little fat kid the next time he came around. Then he remembered about Red Lips and her grandson. He thought about her again, sitting alone on the Wonder Wheel eating her hot dog. She probably had a big red smile and was singing Sinatra to the ghost of Mrs. Manimoskowitz, all that sentimental bullshit she seemed to like so much.

Before he went to mass, Hank found himself standing on the stoop with the virgin. She looked shocked to see him, Netta did, when she came to the door. Like she was not expecting to see him. A moron with a fishing pole.

"For your grandson," Hank said.

"Oh," she said.

"I told him I'd give it to him," Hank said.

Her face went paler than usual. "But he's not here," she said. "He's had to cancel."

"Oh," Hank said. "Does he like fishing?"

She said she didn't know. Then she told him she was going back home to Connecticut where he wasn't too far away, she didn't know what she was thinking, coming back here, and she gave him another story, this one about a man whose wife had been in a plane crash and ended up with amnesia. She couldn't remember anything. Not even her name. Or so she had said. There's always another story, she told him. She said the woman had never really loved her husband, but she'd felt obligated to him. He'd done something once, something secret, nobody knew what it was, but it had saved her from something. Death, maybe. And so she could never leave him, even though she was sure there was someone else out there, someone just for her. But then she was in this plane crash and she survived and she said she couldn't even remember her own name. And it freed her. And she left him. And her life was never the same.

Hank gave Netta the fishing pole and went home to get ready for mass. He saw her through the window in the back bedroom just standing there looking for the birds. Then he found himself on the stoop again. This time, he had a dead Boston fern in a chipped pot in his hands.

"A housewarming gift," he said. "I thought... it's a nice pot, anyway. Maybe you could do something with it. Clean it up a bit. Maybe put some birdseed in it."

"How thoughtful," she said.

"I know it's a little late."

"No, no. Not at all. It's lovely. Thank you."

Hank put Mrs. Manimoskowitz's planter down on the stoop right next to the Virgin Mary. "Maybe she was just a little lonely," he said.

"Who?" said Netta.

"The young lady in the photograph," Hank said.

"Yes," Netta said. "Yes, maybe."

Hank didn't go to mass alone that Sunday, the day the birds were born. What if they had gone to Coney Island together? What if they'd eaten hot dogs and rode on the Wonder Wheel and he'd kept his lunch inside? And what if she told him the secret, the thing that had saved her? He never told his son about the eggs or the amnesiac. It was none of his business. He never saw the little fat kid again. The birds stopped coming and the virgin on the stoop disappeared. And sometimes, on a Friday night, as he sits on the sofa eating his flounder and watching his *Law & Order* in peace, he tells the story again — silently, to himself — the one about Fatty Frankie, and how he'd tossed Fatty his sandwich when he was hiding up there in that tree. Limburger cheese. Hank wasn't going to eat it anyway.

And sometimes, when it's quiet, and the street outside is empty, Hank closes his eyes and listens.

GIRL SCOUT COOKIES

Although a tear
May be ever so near.
~ Nat King Cole
"Smile"

He told her not to hide her cash in the peanut tin, but she did it anyways. He told her it wasn't the last place a crook might look, because sometimes some kinds of crooks get the munchies. Didn't matter they were old and stale. Didn't matter not everyone liked nuts. It was the temptation they couldn't resist, he told her. But she did it anyways.

She was dumb. That's what it was. But the dumbest thing she ever did was when she ordered five boxes of Do-si-dos, knowing full well it was Tagalongs that he liked. Who knows what she was thinking. Her defense was that she wasn't thinking, she just wasn't, that's all. She just did it, without thinking about it, not until the morning the little Girl Scout came knocking on the door with five boxes of the wrong kind of cookies. And then she remembered. But the Girl Scout said it was too late, so she went into the kitchen, climbed on the chair and got into the cabinet above the fridge, pulled out the old peanut tin and paid the Girl Scout for the Do-si-dos. Then she walked into the kitchen with the boxes and said, "Look what I've done."

And that's when he said she'd outdone herself with the stupid. "When have I ever, in thirty-three years, Rita — *thirty-three* — when have I ever eaten a damn Do-si-do?" he said.

"They're just about the same," she said.

"But they ain't the same," he said.

"I'm sorry, Cole," she said. "I just wasn't thinking."

Had she ordered the Tagalongs, he would have rushed home after work and eaten his supper at the table with her just like she likes and then made himself a Sanka and switched on the television. He would have put three or four Tagalongs on a plate. He would have been quite content, sitting in front of the television with the usual cookie and his Friday night shows. Everything would have been fine. But as it was, she'd already told him the little Girl Scout had been and gone, and there was no need to get excited. Then she gave him permission to go over to O'Neill's after work for a drink or two. "You could use a night out," she said.

"Sure, fine," he said. "But who's gonna eat all those Do-si-dos?"

"I'll bring them to the school. They can sell them at the bake sale."

"At what mark-up?" he said. He was getting ready for work, waiting for her to finish ironing his shirt. "Nobody's gonna pay extra for those."

"They'd be the same price," she said. She handed him the shirt. "Careful. It's still hot around the collar."

"Then how will you make a profit? You didn't buy those wholesale. I don't think you can sell those kinds of cookies at a bake sale anyway. That's a resell. You can't do a resell. This shirt's too hot. Are you trying to scald me or something?"

She pulled the latch in the ironing board and it slammed shut. "I'll donate them," she said.

"Jesus Christ, Rita! Why don't you just open up your wallet and hand them twenty bucks?"

"Well what do you suggest I do with them then?"

He sat down and put on his shoes.

"Did you hear me, Cole?" she said. "I asked what I should do with them. If you aren't going to eat them, and I'm not going to eat them, I can't resell them and I can't donate them. What would you like me to do with them?"

"I don't care what you do with them," he said. "Do whatever you want."

When he phoned home on his lunch break to ask what was for dinner, Rita told him she'd decided to give the cookies to Doreen. For the kids. Cole and Rita didn't have kids. Maybe one of them might have liked Do-si-dos. They'd be about thirty now, but still. Doreen said her kids loved them, so that's what she was gonna do.

"That's nice," said Cole. "Just put the meatloaf on a plate and leave it in the oven. I won't be too late."

"I just can't win with you, can I?" she said before hanging up.

After work, he rang her again, just to remind her he wasn't coming home.

"You'll never guess what I've done," she said.

"No, I won't," he said. "So just go ahead and tell

me, will ya?"

"Well, I was on my way to Doreen's with the cookies, but I wasn't thinking…"

"Uh-huh."

"And the bus came, and I got on…"

"Yeah. Get on with it, Rita. This phone call is costing me."

"Hold on a minute. I'm trying to explain. So the bus stops near the school, and I get off…"

"Near the school?"

"And I go in and tell the girl I'm there to donate five boxes of Do-si-dos…"

"What about Doreen?"

"And the girl smiles and says that's nice, so she'll have to ask the principal if it's okay, and I can leave my name and number and she'll call me. So I tell her, no, no, I've got them here. And that's when I realized I must have left them at the bus stop."

"You what?"

"That must be what I did, because when I came home, they weren't here."

"Can we talk about this later, Rita? I'm getting thirsty."

"I've looked everywhere, Cole."

"Well don't get yourself too worked up about them. They're only Do-si-dos."

"That's what you say now," she said. And then she hung up.

It was trivia night at O'Neill's. Cole was the guy who knew crap nobody cared about. He knew how much water a camel could drink, how many times a piece of paper could be folded and how many ridges a dime had. He even knew how much wood a woodchuck could chuck. Rita always found that funny, and if anyone disagreed, she'd let them know they were wrong. Rita didn't take no lip from no one. He would mention that every time it was trivia night at O'Neill's.

"You been staying out of Rita's hair, now you're semi-retired?" said Dale. Dale was a guy Cole knew from around. Not from anyplace in particular. Just around. "That's all they want — just leave them alone." Dale was married to a lady named Carol. That was all Cole could say about her. Carol didn't do too much. At least, not according to Dale.

"Rita's not one of those," said Cole. "She doesn't mind so much if I'm around."

"She will soon enough," said Dale. "They all do."

Cole had already told Dale about the Do-si-dos, but he was regretting it now. What did Dale know about Girl Scout cookies? He thought they all tasted the same.

"It's like this," Dale said. Dale was always saying how it was. "Eventually, they get sick of it. They don't care anymore how you like your eggs. Scramble them yourself, you old goat. Today, it's the wrong cookies. Tomorrow, it's no cookies at all. I retired in May. By June, I was buttering my own toast. They get used to days without you. You're nothing but a nuisance. Keep yourself busy. Stay out of the house."

"I told you," said Cole. "Rita's not your typical broad. She's too smart for that."

Rita may have been too dumb to balance a

checkbook, but she'd never once bounced a check. He'd give her that much. And she could make a pound of chop meat go for a week. Rita was good people. He was good people, too, but only by association. Before her, he was no kind of people at all.

After trivia, Cole headed straight for home. It was Friday. He wouldn't get his Tagalongs, but he could watch *The Tonight Show* before turning in. He expected she'd probably bring up the cookies again. She could go on an on about something for days. That was one thing she had in common with her mother, and she'd always hated the way her mother could do that. Especially near the end, when not much of it made sense or even mattered anymore.

He could still smell the meatloaf in the kitchen. She'd forgotten to put his in the oven like he'd asked. He felt it. It was cold. He turned the oven on and poured a glass of orange soda. That's when he noticed the peanut tin on the counter. It was empty, save a few old bits of dried-up shell. "Now what's she done here?" Cole wondered.

She wasn't upstairs in the bedroom. He checked if all her shoes were there. Her beige slip-ons were missing. He went downstairs and looked for her purse. She usually kept it on a hook inside the coat closet. It wasn't there. Her overcoat was missing too. It wasn't like Rita to go out late on a Friday. Not without telling him. Besides, where did she have to go?

He went into the kitchen and checked on the meatloaf. Maybe she'd come home before Carson. She still called it that, even though he'd been gone for years.

She liked watching it before bed. She wouldn't want to miss that. Not on a Friday.

He finished his meatloaf and put his plate in the dishwasher. He filled the teakettle and put some Sanka into his Hawaii mug with the hula dancer in the green grass skirt. It was too bad she'd left those Do-si-dos at the bus stop. He wouldn't have minded one now.

Carson was on soon. Still no Rita.

It was nearly 12:30 when he noticed the headlights outside. Must be Rita, he thought. The doorbell rang. Must be Rita forgot her keys again, the dingbat.

It was Rita, all right. She'd been crying. There was a police officer there, too, and he was saying, "Is this your husband, Mrs. Sullivan? Is this your house? Are you sure?"

Rita just nodded.

"What's going on?" Cole said. "Rita — where've you been?"

"She's all right, Mr. Sullivan," said the officer. "She's had a bit of an incident, but she's fine."

"I was mugged," said Rita.

"Mugged! Where? What are you doing out this late anyhow?"

"I went over to Doreen's house to drop off the Do-si-dos, and I thought I'd better put that money in the bank like you told me, and it's only over there by Doreen's, you know. How many times did you tell me to do that?"

"The bank shuts at four," said Cole. "What do you mean? I thought you'd left the Do-si-dos at the bus stop."

"What bus stop?" said Rita. "I walked over to Doreen's. I was going to put the money into that machine."

"Just come in and sit down, for Christ's sake, Rita." He took her by the hand and helped her into the house. He noticed how flimsy she'd become. He'd not noticed it before.

"I tried to call you, Cole, but I couldn't remember the number. Can you believe that?"

"Did they hurt you?"

"I don't remember."

"She's still in a bit of a shock," the officer said. Then he explained how she'd ended up down at the station and why it had taken them so long to get her back home.

"They were very patient with me, Cole," said Rita.

"Probably not a good idea for her to be wandering around on her own," said the officer.

"Well thank you for bringing her home, officer," said Cole. "I can take it from here."

Cole made Rita take her shoes off, and then he told her to sit down on the sofa. She was cold. She wanted to keep her coat on. Cole said whatever she wanted was fine. He'd make her a cup of Sanka.

"I'm sorry," she said. "Did I worry you, Cole?"

"I was worried sick, Rita," he said.

"I don't know what I was thinking," she said.

"You've missed Carson."

"Who was on?"

"No one you'd know."

"But still."

"It's okay."

Cole went into the kitchen. He made another cup of Sanka and took it in to Rita.

"It's too bad we don't have any of those Tagalongs now," she said.

"Never mind about the Tagalongs," he said. "How much did they get?"

Rita started to cry.

"Oh, it doesn't matter," said Cole. He sat down next to her on the sofa and put his arms around her. "It's only money," he said.

About the Author

Veronica Turiano was born in Brooklyn and grew up on Long Island. She has a PhD from The University of Manchester and is an Associate Lecturer of English and Creative Writing at Lancaster University. She lives in the English Lake District.